CHARLI HOWARD

Misfit

There's no such thing as normal

PENGUIN BOOKS

PENGUIN BOOKS

UK | USA | Canada | Ireland | Australia
India | New Zealand | South Africa

Penguin Books is part of the Penguin Random House group of companies whose
addresses can be found at global.penguinrandomhouse.com.

www.penguin.co.uk
www.puffin.co.uk
www.ladybird.co.uk

Penguin
Random House
UK

First published in hardback 2018
This paperback edition published 2019

001

Set in 10.61/15.6pt Sabon LT Std
Typeset by Jouve (UK), Milton Keynes
Printed and bound in Great Britain by Clays Ltd, Elcograf S.p.A.

A CIP catalogue record for this book is available from the British Library

ISBN: 978-0-241-32930-6

All correspondence to:
Penguin Books
Penguin Random House Children's
80 Strand, London WC2R ORL

www.greenpenguin.co.uk

MIX
Paper from
responsible sources
FSC® C018179

Penguin Random House is committed to a
sustainable future for our business, our readers
and our planet. This book is made from Forest
Stewardship Council® certified paper.

*To all the girls who have ever
felt their bodies weren't good enough*

CONTENTS

Dear Reader,

Before you start, I just want to warn you about a couple of things. The topics I write about are sensitive and I really want to be honest about my experiences, because I believe talking about things is healthy and we should be able to discuss these matters openly.

However, there is a lot of honesty in *Misfit*. This is a book about my mental illnesses. I use words that I find best express how I'm feeling: mental, cray cray, insane. I know that some people find these words offensive but, for me, it is the best way to talk about my life. So, if you find that problematic, please be aware that you will find words like these in my book.

This is also a book about my eating disorders. I have suffered from both anorexia and bulimia, and I want to talk about them because I am recovering now and passionate about promoting body positivity. But I wasn't always that way, and I have to honestly show what my life was like when I suffered from my eating disorders. I know how certain images, words and phrases can trigger difficult emotions in people suffering from eating disorders, and in people who have suffered from them in the past. I know that people with eating disorders will look for weight-loss inspiration everywhere, and that this book could be one of them. Therefore, be warned: there will be triggers in this book. This was the most truthful way for me to tell my story, but I do not want to cause any harm to others at all – the reason

I have been so honest is to help others who feel a pressure to look a certain way to realize that happiness is not proportional to dress size. If you are suffering or could be triggered, please do not read this book. I'm not a health professional and there is no advice in here. It's all just my experience.

Although all the stories are real, for obvious reasons some names, dates and even locations have been changed. That's because it is my story, not theirs, and I have been respectful of privacy.

Also, when you read this, you will discover that I was quite badly behaved, even as a kid. My teenage years were no better, and there are stories of underage drinking and other stupid things in here. I in no way condone or promote any of this bad behaviour – I was an idiot. Do not try any of these things at home. I really regret them, but have put them in this book because they are part of my story.

These things happened to me and if anything good came out of my experiences it is that I can share my mistakes so that maybe other people don't have to make them too. If it ever seems like I am making light of a situation, please be assured that I'm not – it's just that humour is the best way I know to find light in the darkness. And you can find humour in just about anything. That is my philosophy, but I don't want anyone to be offended by what I've written. This is my personal story, not a self-help book.

If you are suffering, be kind to yourself, and maybe don't read this just yet.

Charli x

No one can make you feel inferior
without your consent.
– Eleanor Roosevelt

PROLOGUE

I am not normal.

From the ages of four to six, I thought I was a dog. A German shepherd, to be precise, though I could also be a Dalmatian, depending on my mood. The dogs I grew up with were spoiled and loved, and played around all day, so that's what I decided I wanted to become. I'd put my hands up to my chest and pretend they were paws, then walk on my tiptoes to mimic the way dogs' feet arch up. I'd squint at things in the distance, the way dogs do when they spot something they're curious about, and growl under my breath at strangers. In fact, I squinted so much that my nursery sent me to an eye specialist because they thought I was going blind. I was *obsessed* with becoming a dog, barking at strangers in the street in the hope they'd mistake me for a real one.

To prove how passionate I was about my alter ego, I spent one Christmas writing countless letters to Father Christmas begging for a metal dog cage I'd seen in the Argos catalogue. I wanted a big one, with room for a few pillows so it would be comfy to sleep in, and space to allow me to grow. Funnily enough, I was disappointed on Christmas morning.

Like many parents, mine thought this was just a phase, until my school genuinely became concerned and wanted me tested for autism. That's when the '*Why can't you just be normal?*' questions began.

I didn't know that wasn't considered to be acceptable behaviour. I was happy pretending to be a dog. In fact, I would go so far to say that I was probably the happiest (and sanest) I've ever been. Since the dog thing, I've had a lot of obsessions. I've been obsessed with germs, believing I've caught HIV from a toilet seat, and wearing gloves on the Tube so I don't touch the poles with bare hands. I have been obsessed with the idea that everyone hates me, working myself up into a frenzy until I want to rip my own hair out.

But, most obsessively of all, I spent almost *twenty years* of my life worrying daily about my weight – nit-picking all my flaws, believing my body to be grotesque, and feeling utterly convinced with every fibre of my being that I was morbidly obese.

My longing to be thin took over my life. To this day, I have never craved or wished for anything so deeply. I wanted to feel the outline of bones underneath my clothes; I wanted people to gasp at my frail frame. Most of all, although I didn't realize it at the time, I wanted people to see I needed help with the anxieties in my brain, without having to actually say the words myself.

To cut a long story short, I know I am a bit mental. I know the word 'mental' isn't a very politically correct term to use, but that's what I am, I suppose. A bit cray cray. I know I don't *look* mental. You wouldn't think I had any of these issues if you saw me on the street, put it that way.

In fact, I have what I like to call 'Sexy Illnesses'. Not because my OCD, depression, anxiety and eating disorders go walking around in fishnets and stilettos, but because they're often glorified and gossiped about in the media or in magazines. You read about a celebrity losing an excessive amount of weight, written in a tone of awed admiration. How many people do you know who have referred to their tidiness as 'OCD', when all they've done is neatly fold their knickers in their drawer? How many people do you know who refer to their PMS mood swings or stressed-out mums as 'bipolar'? These illnesses are talked about as if they're fashionable now, but coping with them is another story.

My story begins at the age of eight, because that was the last time I remember being completely angst-free. Yep, it all went downhill from there, to be honest with you.

Aged eight was the last time I recall feeling like life was simple. I had no idea that periods existed, or that women were treated differently to men, or that my celebrity crush, Ricky Martin, was, in fact, gay. Money grew on trees and people were either fat or thin, black or white, rich or poor. I was, for the most part, totally innocent and naive, with everything a girl could have wished for.

Aged eight was the last time I remember viewing my body as solely that: *a body*. It was the last time I didn't question the way it looked, or view it as though it was Mr Blobby (if you don't know who Mr Blobby is, you're missing out). There was nothing to preen, nothing to alter, nothing to lose. Little did I know it would take nearly twenty years to view it in the same, non-judgemental way as I did back then.

Some people think eating disorders are genetic, and others think they may be caused by the influences around you. Perhaps you were destined to be that way inclined – I certainly had my fair share of mental health illnesses – or perhaps they develop from a build-up of things you see and hear. I personally think it's a bit of both.

My eating disorders were an addiction. I was addicted to being *perfect* – the type of girl other girls want to be. When I saw a series of beautiful, skinny women plastered across fashion magazines and TV, as an impressionable young girl I formed a belief that took me a very, very long time to get over: that to be happy, I had to be thin.

Unlike a lot of people, who can open a magazine and see pictures of thin, beautiful women smizing back at them without so much as another thought, I stored them in a mental filing cabinet. I couldn't forget about them. I managed to convince myself that becoming thin would somehow make all my problems disappear. I mean, if I looked like the girls in magazines, what would there be to be sad about?

You might not be aware of it, but your brain is currently soaking up lots of slogans and pictures without you even realizing. Suddenly, the things you didn't notice about your body before seem *very* noticeable. You're not the same shape as the models you see in magazines. You notice you have acne and cellulite, but those happy girls in adverts would never have flaws like that. For someone with an obsessive personality like me, becoming thin became something else to fret over. I began to hate my body, and wondered how I could possibly change it.

My experience is not unique, I know. It's universal. Think about it. You wake up in the morning and scroll through your Instagram feed, which is full of girls who look like you, just a bit more polished. You leave the house in the morning, drive past a few adverts full of glamorous women having a whale of a time, laughing at things that aren't actually fun, like salad and couscous. After you've finished your food at lunchtime – having battled past so much contradictory dietary advice everywhere you look (*LOW FAT! DELICIOUS! CARB-FREE! BIKINI BOD! INDULGE!*) that you end up hating yourself and whatever you chose to eat – you might flick through a magazine, which features even *more* beautiful women, and whose lives look *far* more thrilling than yours. Later, you make the return journey home, seeing (you've guessed it) more billboards and advertisements. You'll go online and scroll through Facebook or Twitter, clicking (X) on a few weight-loss pop-ups as you go. Afterwards, you'll watch a bit of TV, where women giggle hysterically while eating yoghurt and chocolate in the ad breaks. Then you'll check your phone again before bed, and repeat the same process the next day. And the next. And the one after that . . .

As a teenager, I looked nothing like the girls I pinned on my bedroom wall, but I so desperately wanted to. Their lives were so glamorous and perfect and worry-free. I was chubby and tall – not thin and beautiful like they were. I hated school and felt isolated. They had rock-star boyfriends, tons of money and beautiful clothes, which couldn't have been further from my life if I tried. And so I soon discovered I could plough my anxieties about fitting in and being lonely into controlling what I put in my mouth.

After many years and much soul-searching, these fashion images are what I think triggered my eating problems. At least, in part. As I said, I'm a little bit mad. It could have been a lot of things. Either way, it was after coming to this conclusion from the images around me that I suddenly grew even more concerned about fitting in with the girls in my class. I didn't want the outside to reflect the craziness that was happening up in my head. I was a teenager in the noughties, at the height of the size-zero trend. That was what I thought I needed to look like to be normal.

Maybe if I'd opened up about how I was feeling, my eating disorders wouldn't have been triggered. But if I have learnt anything, it is that people do not like discussing mental health. It freaks them out. And despite the fact that children are capable of developing things like anxiety, eating disorders and depression, it makes grown-ups somewhat uncomfortable. And because we don't like to talk about children's feelings, the domino effect begins, where one undiscussed problem leads to another, and then to another, until children become so overwhelmed that they can't deal with life. At least, that's what happened to me. By the time I was in my late teens I was a seasoned pro at bulimia and starving myself. I was a nightmare at school, acting like a total arse and obsessing over boys. I felt directionless and alone, and thinness was all I could control and therefore all I cared about.

So, how did a slightly bonkers misfit with anorexia, bulimia and anxiety decide to solve her problems? I became a model. As you do.

I truly believed that becoming a model would make my life better. It would mean I was beautiful. It would mean my body was perfect. If I couldn't be 'normal', then I'd be superhuman: the type of girl other girls wanted to be. That was *better* than normal. The people who had ever doubted me or bullied me or called me 'weird' would suddenly want to be my friend. Finally, I'd have a chance of becoming those girls in magazines I'd aspired to be and live the lives they had.

What a prat.

In fact – surprise, surprise – my anorexia and bulimia were exacerbated by modelling. My obsessive personality clung on to the idea that being considered 'beautiful' would make me happy. Over time, my anxieties and self-image got worse and worse. Even when I became really thin I *still* wasn't thin enough. And guess what? Losing weight didn't make me more beautiful, and I certainly didn't end up looking like the girls in magazines.

That's the thing: the girls in magazines don't look like the girls in magazines. Half the time, even *I* didn't look like the overly Photoshopped images I'd had taken of me.

But what better way to prove to the world that I was 'normal' than by hiding my eating disorder behind the glamour of *modelling*! No one needed to know I was making myself sick, or measuring my hips obsessively ten times a day, or falling off running machines from exhaustion. I was becoming the girl I'd dreamt about since my early teens, but as my illness became worse, maintaining the illusion that everything was fine sent me into a meltdown.

It feels insane, looking back now, that I went along with these weird beauty standards. In fact, by working in the industry that partially caused my illness, I was contributing to the problem. It couldn't last, and it didn't. I'm out the other side, and I want to talk about it. I don't want to make the same mistakes again – I want to start a conversation.

This is the story of those missing in-between years, which stretched from my childhood to my mid-twenties, that the pressures of society and pre-existing anxiety conspired to ruin by triggering an obsession with food and thinness. Twenty years of my life that I will never get back. It's a tale of how chasing perfection did not make me happy; how no matter how much weight I lost, I never reached the happiness I wished for. But, most of all, this is how I learnt that there is no such thing as normal, and that standing out is *so much better* than trying to fit in.

1

NOT SO NORMAL

Before we get on to my modelling, or my eating disorders, or even my life as an angst-ridden, anorexic, badly behaved teen, there I was – a relatively normal eight-year-old schoolgirl growing up in 90s Britain. The dog phase had finally ended (thank woof for that) and, like many kids, I had the inner confidence of someone with nothing to lose.

From the day I set foot into the education system it became apparent we would not get along. I hated it till the day I left at eighteen. I hated being confined to a desk all day and being told what to do. I can't work out if that makes me sound like a child genius, far too intelligent to listen to the ramblings of a middle-aged teacher with more life experience than me, or sound as though I had ADHD, although I don't think either is true.

I went to a normal Catholic school in London (despite not being Catholic and despite the fact the local council decided to house registered sex offenders in flats overlooking the playing fields). I had normal friends. I spent plenty of time outdoors. I was a hundred-per-cent content with life.

My dad worked in the navy, which, to me, was normal. The only problem with my dad's job was that we had to move around a lot, often from country to country. By the time I was eight I was on house number five. Moving from place to place and house to house was all I knew. Who was I to question it?

We weren't rich. We weren't poor. We certainly never went without. I knew I was very lucky, even if I did think depriving me of a McDonald's every night was practically child abuse. My parents had normal jobs, and although they had the occasional row they were very much in love and together. My little sister used to wind me up and bite me sometimes, but whose sibling didn't? Bar the odd family drama, life was simple. And, for the most part, I was truly content, except when I didn't get my dog cage for Christmas. Basically, there were no childhood traumas to excuse me from going completely mental later.

One day, my mum and dad announced something.

'We're moving.'

We weren't just moving down the road. We were moving to Germany. To Hamburg, to be precise, which might as well have been the North Pole.

I met this announcement with mixed feelings. It was the first time I had to leave a life I was actually happy with. I'd never had to question how content I was until that moment. This move meant starting over from scratch, when I didn't *want* to start over from scratch.

Moving had never bothered me up until that point, because I'd never had a life I cared so much about. But this time was different. All of my friends were here. It meant coming to terms with the fact that my one true love, Darryl, was probably going to marry someone else while I was away. It meant Kelly was most likely going to forget about me and get a new best friend – probably that cow Kathryn, who had recently begun hanging around us like a bad smell.

Well, I thought, if that was the case, maybe I should move on, too? But wait – what if I never made another friend again? What if I was destined for an entire life of loneliness? This wasn't what I wanted. And, in the annoying way parents decided things without your consent, like dragging you to Ikea for a 'family day out', I had no say on the matter.

My parents went out of their way to convince me that moving would be a great experience for us all. My dad had flown over there to visit the school beforehand, taking photos of it throughout for me to see. The new school looked very fancy indeed – nothing like my school in London. It certainly didn't look like the type of place paedophiles liked to hang around in their free time, or where people stole cars and burned them on the lawn for fun – both of which made a pleasant change. It was a private English-speaking international school in an exclusive part of the city, representing every ethnicity and religion under the sun.

And so we moved. I may have only been eight, but the differences between Hamburg and London were very noticeable. Mainly, the *very* liberal attitude to anything

11

sexual. Billboards were covered in naked women with boobs approximately eleven storeys high. At a sleepover, I was confronted with a massive painting of my friend's parents having sex (I mean, I can't imagine why you *wouldn't* want that in your living room). To get to school, our bus drove down an infamous street full of sex shops and prostitutes. In England, this would have been deemed inappropriate. In Germany, it was fine. For some reason, this barrage of sexual images, words and scenes really affected me. I couldn't look at them without thinking: *SEEEEXXXX!!!!* Could I get pregnant because I was sitting next to a boy on the school bus? Had I had sex with someone without knowing? I was freaking out – and I couldn't help the inappropriate thoughts that popped up when I saw these images.

For the first time I couldn't control what I was thinking – but I knew that what I was thinking was disturbing. From our first week in Germany it drove me absolutely mental.

On the first day of school, I arrived feeling terrified. I was trying to keep it together, but I still missed London and the things I knew. I hastily made my way into the classroom, telling my mum to clear off so as not to embarrass me in front of the other kids.

'I like giving my pupils nicknames,' my new teacher said cheerily once we'd all sat down. 'What's your nickname, Charlotte?'

'I'm not sure,' I replied truthfully, as the class turned to look at me.

'Well, you must have one. Everyone has a nickname! Is it Lottie?' he asked.

'Erm . . . my dad and grandad always call me Charlie,' I said.

'There you go!' he said. 'From now on, you'll be called Charlie.'

So, that was it. It was like a rebirth. For added pizzazz, I decided to drop the 'e' from the end of my name, like a certain Geri 'Ginger Spice' Halliwell. I rather liked the fact that Charli went with my tomboy personality. It may have only been a subtle name change, but this gave me a sense of freedom over my own body – the feeling that I was in control of my own image.

If only I could control my thoughts in the same way. And I don't know if it's coincidental or not – but this was when my bad behaviour started.

By the end of the first week I still hadn't made any friends, and this worried me. I kept daydreaming about Kelly and Darryl, and how they were probably all huddled up with that friend-stealing Kathryn now, laughing at the memory of our marriage and what we once had.

When you're eight, a week of not having a solid friendship group feels like a year, and I knew I couldn't continue life like this. It was far too depressing. So, I decided to take matters into my own hands. I'd make friends in the way I thought best – forming a girl band like the Spice Girls. Who cared that I couldn't sing and that I danced like I was having some sort of fit? With the right band members we could be set for stardom.

I decided to ask two girls in my year I'd been admiring from afar to join – Emma and Hannah. Both were pretty and wore fashionable clothes. Both were avid Spice Girls fans, which made me like them even more. They both also performed dance routines in the playground during break times, and I *desperately* wanted to join in, but didn't feel comfortable enough to ask yet.

So, one Monday break time, I asked (very seriously) if I could speak to them in private. As I stood there, clutching a notepad full of songs I'd written that would *easily* get me noticed as the next Mozart, I took a deep breath:

'Do you want to be in my girl band?'

Emma and Hannah looked at one another.

'Yeah, go on then.'

We recruited another member, Olivia, and by the end of the day we were friends, busy planning what our band name should be. We settled on the Angelz, with a 'z' – because everyone knows adding a 'z' to the end of a name makes things ten times cooler.

Soon, a new girl called Anja joined our class. She was Danish, tanned and beautiful. Without hearing her sing, and despite the fact she could barely speak a word of English, the four of us knew she would make a great fifth member. When Anja became a fully fledged member of the Angelz, our band was complete.

I hadn't got over Kelly, but I did like the fact I now had a nice group of girls to hang around with. Like the Spice Girls, we each had our own personalities:

Emma, who was the most grown-up one, and whose mum let her wear make-up;

Hannah, who looked up to Emma, and who was fun and loyal;

Anja, the pretty one, who had all the boys after her;

Olivia, the academic one, who had issues with her weight;

And me, Charli, the tomboy, who was, as you'll soon discover, the troublemaker.

The third week in, Hannah asked me if I'd like to come for a sleepover – which, in girl land, basically means you're friends.

'Of course!' I said excitedly, as though she'd offered me a million pounds.

Before we went to Hannah's that Friday night, we first needed to make a detour from school to her dentist, where Hannah was going to get her mouth moulded for braces. Braces seemed terribly grown-up. As I waited for her, I looked in the mirror. I hadn't really thought about my teeth before. Were they wonky? Did they make me look less attractive? How had I not noticed that I didn't have straight teeth before?

As I pondered this, I spotted a bowl full of free miniature toothpaste tubes that you could take home with you. Now, I'm not one to pass up a freebie, so I grabbed handfuls of them and shoved them into my pockets, as though the world would suddenly run out of fluoride.

Hannah's house was beautiful and huge, with a big winding staircase and an even bigger garden to play in. Her house was attached to another house owned by an old

German lady called Frau Lardegus, who Hannah had described to me as a horrible old witch. She didn't speak any English, but would routinely tell Hannah's mum in German how irritating Hannah and her brother were, and how she didn't like children, and got them into trouble.

'She sounds awful,' I said. 'We should get revenge on her.'

Hannah's room was the most grown-up room I'd ever seen, with a beaded rainbow curtain across the door frame and a large double bed, which made my room seem terribly babyish in comparison. As an added bonus, she also had her very own balcony that overlooked the sea. Frau Lardegus's room was directly next to hers, with a balcony that was separated from Hannah's by a gap and a large drop.

We had some dinner, then, like any other normal girls, went up to Hannah's room to listen to some music. As I took off my jacket, the toothpaste from earlier suddenly fell out on to the bed.

We looked at each other as though we'd read one another's minds.

'Remember I said we should get revenge . . .?' I asked Hannah, raising an eyebrow.

Now, a psychologist may read the rest of this chapter and think I was being naughty because my life had been uprooted – an act of rebellion, or the need for attention. Looking back now, I think it was probably to distract myself from the revolting sexual images that I couldn't stop from popping into my brain. At the time, I genuinely thought I was doing this on behalf of all the children who had ever been victimized by mean old ladies.

'We need a backpack for our things,' I instructed Hannah, despite the fact that all we were doing was climbing over on to the balcony next door.

She began handing me items we might need for our adventure. Notepad and pen? Check. Spare T-shirt? Check. Brain? Hmm.

'Don't forget this,' Hannah said, handing me her dad's mobile phone. This was at a time when people didn't have mobile phones; they were considered a luxury item, rather than a necessity.

'We don't need that!' I said, and threw it on to the bed.

'What about a hairbrush?' Hannah asked, handing it to me.

'Nah,' I said, and threw it behind me.

CRACK!

The hairbrush smashed the screen of the mobile phone, and Hannah and I looked at each other in shock.

'My dad's gonna kill me,' she said.

Still, there was no time to lose. We could deal with the broken phone another time. We had revenge to get on with. Hannah put the phone on the bedside table, and we put on some jumpers for warmth.

We slid open her balcony door, trying to be as quiet as we possibly could so as not to disturb her parents, who were blissfully watching TV downstairs. I glanced down over the balcony. It was a huge drop. But you don't think about danger when you're eight, so we (stupidly) climbed over the edge and on to the balcony next door. (As a little side note, I'd like to warn readers **DO NOT TRY**

17

THIS AT HOME. Even by my standards, this was pretty idiotic.)

As we peered through the glass and the gap in the curtains, we spotted Frau Lardegus innocently watching TV in her bedroom, with a sewing kit on her lap and dogs by her feet. Anyone would have thought she was a cute old lady. Only we knew the truth.

'Psst, pass me the toothpaste,' I whispered.

Hannah handed me a couple of tubes, which I proceeded to squeeze across the window.

'Let me have a go,' she said enthusiastically, and before long we were like Banksy, fighting the establishment (or mean old ladies) one toothpaste tube at a time.

'Right, I think that's enough,' Hannah said, and we took a step back.

Well, if we'd wanted to make a stand, we'd done a good job of it. The window was covered in the stuff.

As we climbed back over to Hannah's balcony, I was suddenly overwhelmed by a sense of guilt – not to mention fear of how much trouble we'd probably be in when Hannah's mum found out.

'We're gonna have to wipe it off,' I said to Hannah. 'Go and get some toilet paper and wet it, then pass me some over the balcony.'

Suddenly, as we were about to step outside on to the balcony again, there was a knock at Hannah's bedroom door. Our hearts stopped. I shoved the empty toothpaste tubes under the bed as quickly as I could, and we put on smiley, innocent faces as her mum opened the door.

'Having fun?' Hannah's mum asked.

'Er, yeah!' Hannah replied, not daring to look at me.

'Good,' she said. 'OK, darlings, sleep well. I'll see you in the morning! Love you, sweetheart.'

As she closed the bedroom door, not knowing about our random act of anarchy, Hannah looked at me. 'She's going to kill me,' she said. 'We need to get rid of it before Frau Lardegus tells her.'

'Hmm, she's kind of old. Perhaps she's blind and won't be able to see it?' I replied reassuringly.

Hannah went to the bathroom and wet lots of tissue paper, then I climbed back over. She passed me the wet tissue from her balcony and I began scrubbing the window as much as I could.

Now, I'm not sure if you're aware of this, but when you try to scrub toothpaste off glass in a circular motion, it gradually becomes bigger and bigger until it turns into a whiter, smudgier, blurrier mess.

Oh, wait – no, of course you didn't know that, because you're not a f***ing idiot.

'It's not coming off!' I hissed.

No matter how much I scrubbed, it just wouldn't disappear. The window was becoming dirtier and dirtier by the second.

'Maybe it won't look so bad in daylight,' I said to Hannah hopefully, who was panicking by this point. 'It might be a trick of the eyes.'

All of a sudden, Frau Lardegus's dogs began barking hysterically at the window, making her sit up in her chair.

A normal child would have legged it by this point, but as I'm sure you've gathered by now I wasn't normal.

'*Moooo!*' I yelled – yes, like a cow, because why not? – sending the dogs into further hysteria.

'Go, go, go!' Hannah snapped, and I climbed back over the balcony and into her room, sliding the balcony door shut as though none of this had ever happened.

'I don't think the mooing was that necessary,' Hannah said, and to be fair I think she had a point.

'We'll check the toothpaste situation in the morning,' I said, trying to calm Hannah, who was by this stage anything *but* calm. We climbed into bed, hoping that our act of revenge would remain a secret.

Well, all that excitement for one night knocked us out. In fact, it knocked us out so much that we forgot to destroy the evidence – hundreds of empty toothpaste tubes – and were awoken by the sound of Hannah's parents barging into the room.

'*What the hell have you two done?*' Hannah's mum yelled. 'Get out of bed – *now!*'

Oh. The toothpaste must've been noticeable then.

Hannah began crying, her brother was smirking at us in the background, and I stood there not really knowing what to do. I suddenly remembered the remnants of Hannah's dad's now-smashed mobile phone, which lay on top of her bedside table. He must've seen where my eyes were gazing . . .

'*What the hell's happened to my phone!*' he asked angrily, and I tried to do my best 'Oh my, how did that happen?' face.

'Do you know how dangerous climbing over a balcony is?' Hannah's mum yelled. 'You could have both *died*! What on earth were you both thinking?!'

In hindsight, maybe it had been a bit dangerous.

'Your parents are on their way,' Hannah's mum said to me, and to be honest I was pretty grateful for that fact. 'You two are in big, big trouble. This is incredibly unlike you, Hannah.' And then came the worst words a mum can ever say: 'I am very, very disappointed in you.'

We were marched next door to Frau Lardegus's house, where she kept saying how violated she felt, and how she thought she was being attacked by robbers with toothpaste, and how she *definitely* didn't like children now. When my mum picked me up, Hannah's mum began insinuating that it was all my fault, as though Hannah was forcibly made to squirt toothpaste out of a tube and on to a window against her will.

'You couldn't have waited just a few months before putting toothpaste on a window, could you?!' my mum said to me as we drove home. 'We've only just bloody moved here, and look at the impression you've made!'

While getting up to mischief took up the majority of our day, our girl gang also began taking an avid interest in the way we looked, despite the fact we were still only eight years old. We put our musical ambitions on hold to focus on more important things – i.e. make-up, popularity and boys.

Emma was the most fashionable one of the group, the girl I envied the most, and probably the most mature. By 'most mature', I mean she knew about things the rest of us didn't, and was allowed to wear make-up and heels, and read teenage magazines. She may have only had bee stings (because, oh yeah, she was NINE), but her mum had bought her a bra and frilly knickers from M&S that made my white vests and ironing-board-flat chest look very babyish in comparison.

'My sister says boys like big boobs,' Emma informed us knowledgeably.

'I've got the biggest of all of us,' Olivia bragged, and they spent the afternoon bickering about whose non-existent breasts were the biggest.

If Emma said boys liked girls with boobs, she was most probably right. She treated everything her older sister said as though it was gospel. Was this the reason why I couldn't get a boyfriend? Or was it because, as I've said before, I was *a small child*?

For the course of our friendship over the next few years, Emma and Anja got all the male attention, eventually landing the two most good-looking boys in the class. They got Valentine's presents from them and were allowed to go on mini-dates with them at weekends, making Hannah, Olivia and me very jealous indeed. I'd occasionally tried squeezing my boobs together, in a feeble attempt to look like a Page Three model I'd once seen in a newspaper, but I'd never really given my boobs (or lack of them) much thought up until then. But of course, once they start to become the main topic of conversation, suddenly bodies are all you can think about.

So here I was – prepubescent, lanky and already obsessed with my figure.

2

GOD, SEX AND OTHER OBSESSIONS

The more I didn't want to think about sex, the more it flashed up in my head. **SEX. SEX. SEX.** As far as I was concerned, sex was bad, but I was worse for thinking about it. I was eleven, and my bad behaviour was part of my daily life. It was the only way I could distract myself from the chaos in my brain.

Soon the hand-washing started. I genuinely believed I had badness on my hands. If I washed my hands twice before break time, it would make me 'clean': pure from these disgusting thoughts. I'd have lunch, then have to wash them twice again with soap, making sure I got the froth right in between my fingers. But wait – what if I didn't clean them right? What if there was a bit of 'badness' left over on them? OK – time to do it again. Oh God, did I miss a spot? Do it twice again, just to make sure.

As though spending half my life by a sink wasn't enough torture, I spotted a Bible on the bookshelf of my room that had once belonged to my dad. I picked it up and began reading it.

I remembered a priest at my old Catholic school saying God forgave you for your sins no matter what, as long as you prayed for forgiveness and truly meant it. Suddenly it was as though a light bulb went on in my head. This was it. This was the cure to all of my worries, and it had been on my bookshelf all this time. If God knew I was a good person, then I wouldn't have to worry about the thoughts I couldn't control. I'd be good – and who doesn't want to be good?

I began thinking that I'd have to thank God for everything, which became tiresome, but necessary. Every night before bed, I would have to read ten pages of the Bible to show my loyalty towards him, then pray afterwards. Then, if I felt like I hadn't prayed properly, I'd have to do it again and again and again until it felt 'right'.

But it *never* felt right. My efforts were never good enough. I'd sometimes pray until I was so exhausted that I'd fall asleep on my hands still in the praying position. Then I'd have to pray to apologize for not praying properly.

I remember some boys in my class making a jokey comment about something sexual, and me laughing along as though it didn't bother me – because that's what normal kids did: laugh about sex, because it's silly and funny and naughty. I then became consumed by guilt that I'd laughed about something so impure and dirty and *wrong*. God wouldn't believe I was serious about repenting my sins now, would he?

'*I promise I wasn't laughing with them,*' I whispered to myself in a toilet cubicle. '*I was only doing it to look cool, I promise.*'

Sometimes it felt like my brain was purposefully trying to look for things to obsess over, which would then give me an excuse to pray. As soon as I thought of something bad, I started the cycle again. It got to the point where anxiety felt so normal to me that calmness didn't feel right.

In social situations I'd hide my hands under the table so people didn't think I was weird, or would go to the toilets to pray instead. Then I'd have to re-pray for offending God by praying in a public place rather than a church, or for doing it somewhere as gross as a toilet.

I now call it the Brain Deviant, because that feels quite fitting – an evil part of your brain that doesn't want you to be happy, an imaginary demon that clings on to your insecurities and likes to make up weird scenarios in your head to make you feel guilty.

From the outside, you would have never guessed I was dealing with these obsessive, intrusive thoughts. I was the class clown. I was popular. I was invited to every birthday party, every sleepover. Everybody wanted to be my friend. (I'll stop bragging now.) Yet I constantly wore a smile on my face to mask how petrified I was of the cloudy, jumbled mess that was unravelling upstairs in my head. And so, as much as I obsessed about displeasing God, I became equally obsessed with trying to show the world I was a normal girl – one without fears or worries, and one who could have a laugh about normal things. So I tried desperately to hide the anxiety I felt.

Not talking about it is precisely what the Brain Deviant craves. It revels in the fact it drives you crazy. That unsure, anxious energy is feeding it, keeping it happy and alive and bubbling. It leaves you feeling even worse.

I enjoyed the high of doing something 'rebellious', as I called it at the time (aka being a prat), because the excitement helped reduce the constant anxiety I felt. But now I was due another obsession, which, unbeknown to me, would change the course of my entire life.

'I wish I wasn't so fat,' Olivia said with a sigh one day in the playground, squeezing the skin around her waist between her fingers as though it was slime. 'I hate how everyone is so much skinnier than me. No boys fancy me because of how chubby I am.'

'You're not fat,' I said, and genuinely meant it. Yes, Olivia may not have been the smallest girl in our girl group, but it didn't take an expert to see she was far from overweight. But she was utterly paranoid about her weight, and, in turn, she began making me feel paranoid about becoming 'big', too. Compared to the madness in my own brain, it was almost soothing to focus on something as solid as my shape.

'My mum says you and your mum are lucky you're both naturally thin.' She sighed again. 'My mum says you're lucky you can both eat whatever you want and not gain a single pound.'

Now, another person may have disregarded that comment the moment it left Olivia's lips, barely giving it a second thought. But for some reason those words struck a chord, and would stay lodged in the back of my mind for years to come.

Until then, I'd never paid much attention to my body. I didn't know being thin was enviable. In terms of weight, I thought women were either fat or thin – not that you could force your body to be one type or the other. But the way Olivia expressed her jealousy towards my mum and me made me feel special.

Olivia calling me 'thin' gave me a sense of euphoria. I was skinny and lanky at that age. Being complimented on my size was a brand-new feeling – and for the first time in a while I felt happy. It made me feel proud. It felt exciting to be envied for once, when I felt I constantly lived in Anja's and Emma's shadows – the girls who all the boys fancied and who everyone thought were pretty. The only time boys took an interest in me was when I traded them rare Pokémon cards, or joined in on winding teachers up.

High on cloud nine, I went home that night and repeated to my mum what Olivia had told me.

'That's not true,' my mum answered. 'I have to run a lot of miles every week to keep my body healthy. I watch what I eat to stay slim. It takes work.'

My mum and dad have always kept in shape. It feels as though my mum has always had a perfectly flat tummy and thighs that don't touch, while my dad has a six-pack – even now, in his fifties. Growing up, I'd be halfway through a morning kids' TV marathon and they'd have already run miles together, up hills and through woods, for 'fun'. If that's not considered abnormal, I don't know what is.

One summer in Hamburg, our neighbour badly damaged his leg and couldn't run the marathon he'd trained so hard for.

'I'll do it,' my dad offered.

And so he did. He hadn't trained a single minute for it, yet ran the entire twenty-six miles without missing a beat.

Although I'm not a fitness fanatic like my parents, no one on either side of my family is overweight, so the chances of me becoming 'fat' has always been quite slim (as it were). Aged eleven, I was like a human bin. I could eat as many biscuits and chocolates and crisps as I wanted and still look like a stick.

That doesn't mean my sister and I lived off junk, though. Far from it. Treats were kept out of reach, although we would climb on to the kitchen worktop to steal a biscuit or two when no one was looking. Dinners were always balanced and healthy, and my lunch boxes even more so, which made me crave fizzy drinks and chocolate like the other kids in my class had, whose lunch boxes were far more exciting and E-number driven.

When you look at photos of skinny models or celebrities it's easy to assume thinness comes naturally to them. But as I learnt a few years later, my mum was right. For the majority of us females, being thin *does* take work. We are designed to store a bit of meat on our bones. And even if you are naturally slight, it doesn't make you any more or less 'lucky' than somebody else. I just wish Olivia could've seen that – or that her mum could've praised her daughter instead of passing on the baton of body image issues to the next generation.

After that, thinness became a regular topic of conversation. Emma would point at older girls in the canteen and comment on how thin they were. She'd say she wished she had a figure like mine. It makes me sad that talking about bodies became 'normal', when we should have just been having fun. We were *eleven*.

Olivia moaned constantly about how fat she felt, or how someone had called her fat, or how her mum had told her the puppy fat would eventually come off. The more she spoke about it, the more frightened I became of getting fat, too.

I voiced my concerns to Mum, who looked at me as though I was mad. I could never be fat, she said, because we didn't come from a big family. I only needed to look at my grandparents' bone structures to see that. But I wasn't convinced.

The word 'fat' had such negative connotations, and I could see how upset and ashamed it made Olivia feel. It would take one 'You're fat!' slur by some immature arsehole in the playground to ruin her entire week. People used it to put girls down. It was easy for boys to call Olivia fat when they knew it would strike a nerve with her, even though it wasn't true – and if it had been, so what!

Any of the older kids considered fat were ridiculed, and

Olivia didn't want to become that. Fat meant lazy. It meant no boys fancied you. It meant unpopular. It meant a series of things that I didn't want to be.

The Angelz were now the most popular group in primary school. At least, that's what Emma said, who'd learnt about popularity from her older sister. Although I wasn't an expert in the dictionary definition of the term, I'm pretty sure she actually meant 'cool'.

Emma was becoming far more competitive as time went on. She began placing us in order of popularity, or beauty, or intelligence. According to her, Anja was the prettiest, then her, then me, then Olivia, then Hannah. She also, apparently, ranked quite high in the 'popularity' stakes, though I did come second to her, which was better than being bottom, I suppose.

I began getting annoyed with all of this nonsense, but it was difficult to argue with her because she was still my friend. Even though she would say mean things occasionally, I still would have preferred to have her as a friend and be part of the Angelz than lose her. We may have been the most 'popular' girls in our school, but there were still tiers of popularity in the group to abide by as well.

For example, if one girl wore glitter on the side of her face, you wouldn't be allowed to wear it in the same place. If more than one girl fancied the same boy, it would become a war over who was 'allowed' to 'have' him. If one girl had her birthday at a bowling alley, another girl would have to book elsewhere. The rules were very complicated indeed.

*

Apparently I was getting too 'out of hand' and 'badly behaved'. My parents were warned by the school that one more step out of line would see me expelled. It was all small stuff – pranks on teachers, disrupting lessons. But it was enough to zone the Brain Deviant out – and all my misdemeanours were adding up.

Our year group was due to go on a school trip to the planetarium. We were all excited to stretch our legs outside school – or, as I liked to call it, 'prison'.

The day started off well. The forty or so students in our year made our way to the U-Bahn (the German Underground), and we were told to be on our best behaviour because we were 'representing the school'.

Trains are boring, aren't they? In fact, this whole school trip was boring, and we hadn't even started it yet. I glanced around the carriage at the boring teachers and boring classmates and boring view and boring . . .

But wait. What was that?

It was a button. A big, shiny red button, with 'EMERGENCY STOP' written above it in German, along with some other funny words. It was practically calling out to me. I couldn't ignore it.

SCREEEEECCHHHHHH!!

The train pulled to a halt, and everyone on it began muttering and mumbling, trying to work out what had happened. An announcement was made over the tannoy and the train pulled very slowly into the platform. The driver came all the way down to our carriage, peering inside and then shaking his head once he saw a bunch of kids.

'Who set off the alarm?' our teacher said, and everyone looked around. The thing is, no one actually knew. I'd done it when everybody's backs were turned.

'What an idiotic thing to do,' she said. 'There's a one-thousand-mark fine for that.'

Although I was young, I knew that was a *lot* of money.

'Was that you?' Emma hissed once the teacher had looked away, and the rest of the Angelz looked at me with wide eyes.

'Er . . . yes,' I said, and suddenly realized how stupid I'd been. 'Do you reckon they'll know it was me?'

'Duh!' Hannah said. 'You're the naughtiest person in the class!'

'I'm sure it will be fine. Just don't tell anyone,' Anja said, and the Angelz vowed to keep it between ourselves.

But then some teacher's pet overheard what we'd said and told on me. The next morning I was hoisted into the headmaster's office.

This time, I knew I was in big trouble. So I lied and said I couldn't remember pushing it.

'What do you mean, you "can't remember"?' the head-master said, confused. 'You either pushed it, or you didn't.'

'I . . . I really don't know if I did,' I replied, feeling scared. 'I might have done, I might not. I honestly can't remember.'

The headmaster made a few phone calls.

'Wait here,' he said, and left the room.

A few minutes later, which felt like forever in child land, the headmaster walked in with a twee-looking lady wearing glasses.

'This is Miss King,' he said. 'And she's a counsellor.'

The counsellor sat opposite me with a sympathetic look on her face, or, more accurately, the face you give mental children you're trying to analyse.

'We've been talking, and the school is going to arrange counselling sessions once a week to get over this bad behaviour,' she said.

'That's OK,' I replied, thanking her for the thought. 'I'm actually fine now. I won't do it again.'

'It doesn't work like that,' she said. 'We need to understand what's making you behave this badly.'

From then on, every Tuesday, I'd get to skip maths (yay) and make my way to the counsellor's office (boo) where we discussed my 'feelings'.

'Now, Charlotte,' she said during our first session in a patronizing tone. 'Apparently you can't remember pushing the emergency button on the train?'

'Yep. Well, no. No, I can't.'

'Hmm.' It was quite obvious I was lying. I'm the worst liar in the world. *Scribble, scribble, scribble.* I tried to glance at what she was writing in her notepad.

'You quite clearly have an obsession with misbehaving,' she said. 'Why do you do it? Are there problems at home?'

Well, why did she think I did it? I was hardly Stephen Hawking but it didn't take a genius to work out it was quite clearly for fun, did it?

'Because it's fun?' I replied, like she was the crazy one.

'Hmm,' she said again, jotting it down in the notepad. 'I don't think it's fun at all. It's actually very silly. It's like a compulsion.'

I didn't realize counselling came with a series of lectures, too. I would've rather endured maths, if I'm being honest. Besides, a lot of our sessions felt like a guessing game. If I said something she didn't like, she made me feel like I was in trouble. So I'd second-guess what she expected me to say, even if it wasn't how I truly felt, so she would tell me what a great counselling session we'd had at the end. I didn't want her to think I was mental.

'Who do you think is thinner – Charli or Anja?' Olivia asked Emma and Hannah in the playground one afternoon. I didn't think there was much difference between Anja and me, and once again I was confused about why she was judging us.

'Anja,' Emma and Hannah replied without missing a beat.

'I thought I was . . .?' I replied, hurt. I felt inadequate, but also silly for caring about it to begin with.

'You're not the thinnest,' Emma said, knocking me off my perch. 'Anja definitely is.'

I began feeling flustered and irritated. 'What do you mean?'

'Stand next to each other,' Emma ordered bossily. Using her hands as a measuring tape, Emma proved me wrong.

'See?' she said. 'Anja's the thinnest. Then you. Then me, then Hannah, and then Olivia.'

It may have only been by centimetres, but it was one more thing that Anja had that I didn't. Anja was beautiful. She had a rich family. She had hordes of boys fighting over her. I couldn't dislike her, because on top of those things, she was a wonderfully sweet and caring friend (ugh). But now, the one thing that made me enviable had been snatched out of my hands.

'See!' Olivia said, getting visibly upset. 'I told you I was the fattest one!' She was almost in tears. Olivia was desperate not to be fat in any way, shape or form, like it was worse than death or something.

I didn't like being lined up like I was in some sort of cattle ranch. I didn't like how Olivia was now even *more* insecure about herself, when I spent what felt like my whole life convincing her that her body was fine. But most of all, I didn't like being in the middle of 'thin' and 'fat'.

Once again, I didn't stand out. I was average. There was nothing special about me after all. Perhaps if I was the thinnest – smaller than Anja – I'd be considered the prettiest. We may have only been eleven, but I suddenly knew what I wanted to be.

Thin.

3

THIN BUT DEFINITELY NOT 'IN'

I wasn't an idiot. I knew we had to move at some stage in our lives. That was just a by-product of having a dad who worked in the military. I just didn't know it would be so sudden.

We were moving to Belgium, and my parents once again assured me I'd be happy. I wasn't too sure about that. How could I beat the friendship group I had in Germany? And what was the effin' point of settling in anywhere if we had to move every couple of years?

My last day of school was filled with tears. I sobbed in the classroom as we took our final lessons, despite having hated them before. I sobbed as Emma's mum took the final photos of us as the Angelz. I sobbed as I made my final walk past the counsellor's office. I sobbed on the bus home until my eyes became swollen and red. I was completely and utterly heartbroken.

In fact, I sobbed for weeks. How was I ever going to get over this feeling? I'd never felt this low before.

I may have only been twelve, but I knew I was going to hate Belgium.

I'm pretty grateful social media didn't really exist when I was twelve, so I didn't see what Emma, Anja, Olivia and Hannah were doing back in Germany, or what party I hadn't been invited to. If I had, I don't know how I would've coped. It's bad enough for my anxiety now.

Belgium was as rubbish as I'd expected it to be. When you've left somewhere as bright and flamboyant as Hamburg to move to a small town in the middle of nowhere, where the local tongue is Flemish, you'd probably be understandably p*ssed off yourself. Everything was either grey, beige or brown, and, no, that is not an exaggeration. They did excel at one thing, and that's Belgian frites, but that's about it.

Our house was a small brown bungalow, and no one on our street spoke a word of English. There was an old lady across the road who, over the next few weeks, seemed to develop a bit of a crush on my dad, but while she was friendly enough she wasn't exactly someone I could have a sleepover with.

In order to have a sleepover I needed friends, and in order to make friends I needed to go to school. My anxiety began to ramp up again, and I began desperately praying I'd be able to fit in, like I had easily done in

Hamburg. My parents assured me I'd make friends in no time.

Spoiler alert: I didn't.

There was only one English-speaking school for miles around, and due to the large amount of American military personnel based there it happened to be an American high school. I was one of just three British people in a school of over a thousand pupils, making me an oddity. Not only that, but because of the way the education system differed to ours I'd now be a year ahead of myself. In teenage land, this was a big deal – a one-year age gap between twelve- and thirteen-year-olds may as well be ten. What a way to start secondary school, eh?

This school was *rough*. Girls would tattoo and pierce each other in the toilets, an offer I turned down many a time. There was a fight practically every day, where girls would often rip each other's hair out on the lawn. One day, I even found a used condom on the floor, which as you can imagine was a truly delightful sight.

I spent a lot of time daydreaming about the good ol' days with the Angelz, and wondering what they were now up to. Did they miss me? Were they still my friends? I'd tried calling them a few times on the landline, but I'd often be greeted with 'They're out playing volleyball/at a party/at a sleepover' or 'I'll get her to call you when she's back', which they rarely did. I couldn't understand how, after promising to stay the bestest of friends forever and ever, it was as though I no longer existed.

'You need to try and move on and make new friends,' my mum would say, and she was right. But I just couldn't.

I was sitting in gym class early in the term when a skinny Spanish girl came and sat in front of me. I'd never seen anyone so thin before – she was skinnier than Anja, and that's saying something. Like Anja, she had oodles of boys fawning over her like she was some sort of exotic goddess. I watched as she happily bathed in the attention, desperately wishing I was as popular as her – before remembering I was the plankton at the bottom of the food chain, and the chances of me ever getting a boyfriend were slim to none. Aside from the time she taught me key swear words in Spanish, we didn't have much communication over the next year, though that didn't mean I couldn't ogle her when she wasn't looking.

She had dimples above her lower back because of how thin she was, and, like a psycho, I weirdly began hoping her gym trousers would fall lower that day so I could study them more closely. She looked so frail and delicate. From the front, her hip bones jutted above her tracksuit bottoms. Her wrists looked like they could snap at any moment.

Thin, thin, thin. I couldn't prise my eyes away from her body, no matter how hard I tried.

Maybe I was looking too much into things, but I soon spotted a common theme between Anja and the Spanish Girl. They were both pretty. They were both popular. They were both sexual goddesses (apparently). And it could've been mere coincidence, but they both happened to be T-H-I-N. Was this the magic ingredient for fitting in?

Being thin was not only a beauty ideal in my eyes, but also a way of being. This was the early noughties, and I was on the brink of becoming a teenage girl. Everything I read or saw surrounded the notion of women being thin, and not much else. Women tried to get rid of their curves, as though they were somehow grotesque. Magazines and the media encouraged you to lose weight, repeatedly picturing the same white, skinny models and celebrities across their pages – and, in turn, making you feel as though you had to look that way, too. This is precisely what I'd do – mentally link popularity with thinness.

'Are you a lesbian?' some guy yelled at me one day in front of his friends, waking me up from my intense ogling of Spanish Girl. Although being a lesbian is far from an insult, I glanced down at my lap, mortified. This boy was called David. He was allegedly the most popular boy in the year and dated the most popular girl, despite the fact that he resembled an unwell, anaemic rat and barely came up to my shoulder. From the moment I'd arrived at the school he'd taken a great dislike to me, and I still have no idea why, other than I was different.

Some people say that if a boy is mean to you, it means he fancies you. I can categorically tell you that if a boy is mean to you, it's because he's a dick. Don't let anyone treat you badly under the illusion it's a crush. You deserve so much better than that.

David would spit at me. He'd push me into lockers, despite the fact I was quite little. He'd tell me girls were going to beat me up, despite the fact I'd never had any issues with anyone before. He'd call me ugly, make fun of my flat chest, or make weird, sneery voices at me, which were kind of creepy. I began to hide whenever I saw him, terrified of what he and his friends might do to me that day.

In an effort to impress him, the popular girls would then start being horrible to me, too – throwing food at me across the dining room, or calling me ugly or whatever other original insult they could think of. Someone made up rumours about how I fancied certain boys in my year and scribbled them all over the walls of the girls' toilets. And I'd just sit there and take it, too frightened of what would happen if I argued back.

We'd been living in Belgium for a few months and I still hadn't settled in. It was miserable, feeling like I didn't have a single friend. Lunchtimes were spent huddled away in a corner of the library, hiding from the librarian, who also seemed to hate me, or sometimes not eating at all. If it meant having to eat in the canteen, where I was guaranteed a sh*tshow, I refused to go in.

Over time the desire to skip school altogether grew stronger. I'd do that sometimes – deciding to walk round the local shops instead, or spend long periods of time in the toilets away from everyone. I was just so sad.

This wasn't the type of sadness you experience if you miss a loved one, or when you accidentally burn a pizza in the oven. This was a sadness that crept up on me, a feeling I simply couldn't shake. Nothing made me happy. It was a sadness that made me feel too tired to get up in the mornings, and which would send me to bed early every night. When it was dark I would cry and cry until I physically couldn't any more, the insides of my body feeling like weights that were pulling me down into the mattress.

Eventually, my overwhelming sense of sadness turned to not caring about a single thing. My body was too exhausted to feel anxious any more, too exhausted to feed my nervousness.

My mum put it down to hormones in the beginning, I think. When I found it hard to get up in the mornings I guess she thought I was being difficult. I couldn't bring myself to tell her I'd considered dying. I didn't want to lumber her with my problems. I'd often made comments about how I didn't want to go to school, but I'd been saying that my entire life. What was new there?

Bedtime became my sanctuary and safety net. I felt calm in the dark where no one could hurt me or make fun of me. I felt at peace. No worries, no bullies. I was left alone and that's how I liked it.

And that is how my depression started, although I didn't know what it was at the time.

Some people call depression 'the black dog', which has never really resonated with me. I love dogs, and comparing something as awful as depression to them doesn't seem that fair, does it?

This is how I describe it. Imagine that on a regular, happy day you are surrounded by an almost-clear cloud. Over time, as your thoughts become more negative by the day and the depression worsens, the cloud becomes greyer in colour. Every negative thought turns the cloud greyer and greyer, darker and darker, heavier and heavier, like a fog. This fog makes your mind fuzzy: you can't think clearly, let alone see clearly.

At your lowest point the fog is so thick and dark and heavy that you can no longer see anything. No matter how hard you fight, you feel lost in this smog and unable to shake it off. I was stuck in an abyss with no way out.

The final straw for me came towards the end of the academic year. I was sitting on the floor in gym class when David threw a basketball at me as hard as he could. I don't need to tell you that it *f***ing hurt*. My eyes began to well up – not only through embarrassment, but also in pain.

'F***ing idiot,' he said, and strolled off with his friends like that was a normal thing to have done.

I left the gym and punched my locker as hard as I could repeatedly. I cried and cried and cried. 'I can't stay here another year,' I kept saying to myself through my sobs. I honestly didn't know how I could've survived it.

The class had yet to finish, but I went into a toilet cubicle to hide and didn't come out for the rest of it. Someone came in and asked if I was OK, but I lied and said I was fine.

But I was sick of pretending I was fine. I just wished someone knew how un-fine I truly was.

*

Sometimes when you're so caught up in your own worries and struggles, you don't feel like anyone cares. But someone always does.

Unbeknown to me, my parents had been searching for alternative schools almost the entire year I was there. However, in order to do that, it would mean changing our family's whole dynamic. If there'd been a better school to send me to in Belgium, I would've gone there instead. But there wasn't.

There was one other option: a very expensive all-girls boarding school near to my grandparents in England. Going to boarding school was never supposed to be part of my story, but it *would* give me a chance to be less miserable.

'I didn't give birth to you only to send you away,' my mum told me recently and, although I didn't see it at the time, boarding school was her only way of saving me.

It would stretch my parents financially, but if it meant me getting a better education and being happy, it was better than nothing.

My parents showed me a brochure of the school, which looked like a fairy tale compared to the school I was in. Then again, North Korea would have looked appealing by that point. I still wasn't a hundred-per-cent sold on the idea, but anything was better than what I was currently dealing with.

It was worth a try – and, hey, if I didn't like it, I was certain I'd only have to endure it for a couple of years at most, just like I had all the other schools.

4

THE MAKINGS OF A MISFIT

If you've ever questioned whether boarding school is like Harry Potter, then you're right – it's not. I'd had high hopes for my new Hogwarts-esque future, but it couldn't have been further from that if I'd tried. There were no owls, although you could keep a pet hamster in the Pet Hut (i.e. an insulated shed opposite the IT block). There was no potion-making, although I did get into trouble for deliberately melting a series of plastic rulers with a Bunsen burner. In fact, I think the closest we ever got to magic was putting lacrosse sticks between our legs and humming the Harry Potter theme tune, while running across the sports field to the sound of our PE teacher yelling.

In fact, boarding school wasn't what I expected it to be at all. The brochure made it seem like something out of an Enid Blyton novel, when in reality it was just a school you lived and studied at. For someone who hated school with a passion like I did, you might as well have chucked me in Guantanamo Bay.

Going to a new school is tough enough as it is. But now, with the added bonus of having reached puberty before the majority of the other girls in my class, I was sure to be a certified misfit. And, for someone who wanted to blend in and be accepted, all I seemed to do was stand out.

Periods, to me, were **THE SINGLE MOST EMBAR-RASSING THING EVER.** Needless to say, I didn't want to talk about them. I didn't want to even hear the word. I couldn't believe that being female came with all this gross and unnecessary baggage.

As though having to start a new school wasn't terrifying enough, I'd recently started my period, so I now had the added pleasure of having to deal with bleeding and cramps on my own . . . as well as showering, clothing and feeding myself. It was an awful lot to handle.

'Don't worry,' my mum said, 'there'll be lots of girls in your year who have started theirs.'

On the day I arrived to unpack my things and settle into my new school, dressed head-to-toe in denim (thanks, Mum), the atmosphere in my family could only be described as depressing AF. Honestly, it was like my family were going into mourning, acting as though I was never going to return. My mum was telling me to fold my clothes and hang my uniform up properly at night. I began Blu-Tacking a few magazine clippings on to the wall in an attempt to make my dorm, which I was now sharing with a stranger, a bit cosier. From the outside I may have been holding it together, but I was absolutely petrified of being on my own – and most of all, about potentially being bullied again.

I thrust the slightly unnecessary amount of sanitary-towel packets my mum had bought me to the back of my wardrobe in shame, before my dad saw. I was terrified at the thought of having to deal with something so grown-up on my own. What if I leaked in my knickers or on the bed sheets like I had before? How would I be able to hide the stains or wash the blood out without anyone noticing? My mum had always been there to help me with that, and now here I was stuck in a school in the middle of the Welsh countryside with a lot of responsibility for myself. I mean, I still read the *Beano* and played my Game Boy, for God's sake.

'Now, if anyone gives you any grief, you punch them in the face,' my dad said, which, in hindsight, probably wasn't the greatest advice. As I watched my mum and dad drive away that Sunday afternoon I burst into tears. I just wished I'd pretended life was hunky-dory at my old school and got on with the bullying back in Belgium. The only upside was that my nan and grandad lived fifteen minutes down the road, meaning I could go and stay with them at weekends if I wanted to.

'You dress weird,' one girl said to me that night at dinner. I looked down at my outfit, then back at what the other girls were wearing. Perhaps they had a point. The girls around me were all dressed in fashionable clothes from Topshop – not this denim get-up that made me look like a deranged cowboy from 1974.

Over the first few days I soon discovered I was one of only three girls in Year 8 who had started their periods. Three. *Great*. Thanks, Mum, you were wrong. And bleeding out of my bits wasn't the only thing that made me stand out.

The first problem was my accent. My voice wasn't posh like theirs. I still had a lingering south London accent, *for Gawd's sayke*. I didn't have ponies roaming around in my back garden. My shoes weren't cool enough. In fact, everything that I thought of as normal was apparently wrong.

Compared to the other girls in my year, I was also a huge, furry monster. I'd peek enviously at the other girls getting changed and see their smooth skin and flat chests that had yet to be blessed by puberty. I had hair on my legs, on my bikini line and underneath my arms – not to mention the two caterpillars some may call 'eyebrows' plastered across my face, which made me look like the female equivalent of Liam Gallagher. No matter how often I shaved my underarms, the hair would grow back within a couple of days, and I wished I looked as lithe and as young as the rest of the girls still did.

My body looked completely different to theirs. As they stretched, I saw ribcages. You couldn't see a hint of bone underneath my skin – I had rolls on either side of my body and looked so *squishy* in comparison, a bit like a slug with arms. I hated my body for having developed so early.

*

Because I went home every weekend without fail, my nan and I became the best of friends. I adored spending time with her. There was no one who quite understood me the way she did. We laughed at the same things. We both loved animals. We both fancied Simon Cowell. She never told me off – if anything, she repeatedly told me how wonderful I was, which made a pleasant change from being told I was naughty. I loved her hugs, her cooking, even the way she tucked me into bed. I never took going home for granted.

Staying in school for five nights a week was proving too difficult. I couldn't cope with the homesickness, and became moody and binged on junk food constantly. It was just typical teenage behaviour, but weirdly I'd stop acting up every time I went home to my grandparents.

Eventually, and much to my housemistress's disapproval, I started going home every Wednesday night, too, to help break up the weeks. My heart would race with excitement when I saw my grandparents' car pull up into the driveway.

I began counting the days down to weekends obsessively, crossing off the days on my calendar like I would in anticipation of a holiday. A lot of this excitement boiled down to the fact I was absolutely spoiled rotten. In an attempt to make my room at their house feel more homely, my nan and grandad went out and bought furnishings for it – a crystal lamp shade, pink curtains and bubblegum-pink paint.

A major way in which my nan expressed her love was through food and feeding people. This was understandable: she grew up during the Second World War, at a time when food was rationed, and so feeding me was a way of taking care of me and showing me I was loved. Considering my mum is very much into healthy eating and force-fed me salads every night (child abuse), this was amazing.

Each Saturday, my nan and I would have our lunch out in town, laughing over cups of tea and gossiping about celebrities. After a day of shopping, she'd then order us a takeaway in the evening and we'd sit down to watch *The X Factor*.

Food, food, food.

It became a friend. I began living for the rich, sugary, salty, buttery deliciousness of it. Food didn't judge you in any way. If anything, it made you feel better, gave you a lift. Food made my school days slightly more bearable, even if all I was eating was carbs, sugar and junk.

I was eating my feelings and didn't regret a second of it. Homesick? Eat. Sad? Eat. Lonely? Nothing a packet of McCoy's ridged beef-flavoured crisps couldn't solve! Every slice of pizza, piece of chocolate or can of fizzy drink comforted me, leaving me feeling warm and fuzzy on the inside, even if it was just until my next meal. I'd have two, three rounds of school dinners, loading up on bread and none of the healthy stuff (I mean, you can't get high off lettuce, can you?).

I couldn't eat until I felt satisfied, though. Oh no. I had to eat and eat until the button on my jeans wouldn't do up, or until I couldn't move. Then, even if I was still full by that stage, I'd eat some more.

Before my grandad drove me back to school, my nan would hand me a plastic bag full of chocolate bars, crisps and cans of Diet Coke, which she told me was to be spread out until I next came home. She didn't know it, but this bag would usually be empty within a day. I'd then go to the school's tuck shop and buy even *more* junk food, eating and eating until I felt physically sick. Nobody stopped me from this obsessive eating, and not many twelve-year-olds are known for their self-restraint.

I avoided looking at myself in the mirror. I absolutely detested my appearance. I hated how my eyebrows were too big. I hated how I towered above everybody else. Yet I still had the mentality that I could eat anything I wanted and wouldn't gain a single pound.

I ranked pretty high on the Freak-O-Meter. Not only was I the unfashionable, chubby and tall new girl, but I was also the unfashionable, chubby and tall new girl who had (shock horror!) periods.

To my fellow twelve-year-old classmates who hadn't started theirs yet the idea of blood coming out of a vagina was hilarious, terrifying and very weird. A few girls would ask me about periods out of curiosity, as though I was some kind of agony aunt from *Mizz*, when I didn't really know what was going on with my body myself. Although I'd been told periods were a natural sign of being a woman, I still felt like some kind of oddity, and I didn't like the way puberty made me stand out.

Despite my best attempts at female bonding, the other two girls in my class who had started didn't want to discuss their periods with me out of embarrassment, which made me feel even more like periods were something to be ashamed of. With no one to talk to, I felt totally on my own. And so I decided to hide my periods as much as I possibly could.

My cramps were absolutely *excruciating*. Not only that, but they could come on at very inappropriate moments. There were a good few times when my period was so heavy I'd leak through my knickers and on to my school skirt, and I'd furiously wash the blood out in the bathroom basins before anyone could see. Another time, at breakfast, I suddenly felt a cramp and just knew it had come on. I could feel the dampness between my thighs and didn't know how I was possibly going to change my school skirt without people noticing. Luckily, I managed to tie my grey school cardigan round my waist, ease my way backwards out of the canteen, then run across the grass and straight back to my room.

Instead of asking for help, I spent the first few terms in absolute agony. I was convinced nobody else knew what I was going through and that women just didn't talk about these things.

But trying to be discreet about my period was very difficult indeed. Sanitary towels, as I soon found out, make **THE LOUDEST NOISE KNOWN TO (WO)MAN** when opening them in a cubicle, so I'd often wait for a toilet to flush before unwrapping the packet quickly. And don't get me started on tampons. The idea of sticking those – no, screw that, *anything* – up my hoo-hah terrified me more than umbrellas (yes, I have a phobia of umbrellas. I don't trust their spiky edges).

Just a few weeks into boarding school, somebody left a drop of blood on the toilet seat without wiping it away. Suddenly, our class became embroiled in the Period Drop Scandal, trying to discover who the culprit could be. No one wanted to wipe the blood away themselves or use the cubicle, as though it had been somehow cursed by the Devil, which meant some poor cleaner had to do it for us. For a good few days this drop of blood became a whodunnit mystery, and I became one of the prime suspects.

'But my period isn't even on,' I said to the jury. Some of the less informed girls looked back at me, clueless, not realizing that your period only comes once every four to six weeks. One girl, for example, assumed that when your period started, it was going to happen every day for the rest of your life (God, can you *imagine*?). When it came to the female body, compared to other girls in my class, I was some kind of wise master. The Vaginal Dalai Lama.

I didn't enjoy this unwanted attention. I wanted to hide my body more than ever. I began wearing baggier things, feeling too ugly to wear fashionable clothes like the other girls. I may not have looked cool, but at least I was hiding the new womanly body I wasn't prepared for.

As the weeks went on, I couldn't understand why I wasn't settling in. No matter how hard I tried to distract myself from home, I just couldn't. Five nights a week at school felt too much, and speaking to my mum and dad on the phone made things ten times worse. The Brain Deviant liked to tell me that they had sent me here because they didn't love me, flashing up images of my mum, dad and sister snuggled up together on the couch, having fun as a family without me around to ruin it.

My great-grandmother, Nanny Beckett, also happened to live near my school on a council estate, and my nan would make me visit her every weekend without fail. It was an odd contrast, leaving a wealthy school surrounding to visit an estate where families were really struggling.

Visiting my great-grandmother wasn't exactly a bundle of laughs. I'd sit in the living room watching TV while my nan put Nanny Beckett's hair into rollers, narrowly avoiding the scratches of her feral (and slightly mental) cat.

Nanny Beckett had had a tough life. She'd left the bright lights of London after the war to move up north with my great-grandad, whose family all lived up there. She dreamt of performing in shows and travelling the world singing, but this was at a time when you did what your husband said, and after a few factory jobs she ended up working in a launderette for a while. I always knew that I didn't want a life littered with regrets about not having followed my dreams – or one where I followed a man.

I can't recall a time in my life when Nanny Beckett didn't have OCD. When I was little she was admitted to a psychiatric hospital, after persuading herself she was dying of imaginary illnesses like brain tumours or cancer. A headache would convince her she was dying. Doctors offered her tablets and therapy to help with her OCD, but she refused any help given her. Eventually, she managed to convince doctors she was OK and was discharged.

Nanny Beckett's living-room drawers were filled with notepads of handwritten, utterly useless information, which had been scribbled all over in blue and black ink. After becoming paranoid that she was losing her memory, she felt she needed to write down everything she'd read or seen so that she wouldn't forget things.

For example, she couldn't watch *Coronation Street* without writing down the entire episode and what had happened between all of the characters. If she met someone in the street, she had to write down all their news and gossip. If the news came on, she'd have to write down all the headlines. One time, she even went through a stage of writing down the licence plates belonging to people on her estate, until some man started yelling at her, thinking she was reporting him for parking illegally.

If she remembered things and wasn't in reach of her notepad, she'd scribble all over her palms and the back of her hands. Her hands were once so blue with ink that I thought she'd got hypothermia, and had to do a double take. If I questioned her about the ink on her hands, she'd pull her sleeves down and cover it up. It was as though she knew what she was doing was crazy, but she just couldn't stop herself.

When her TV broke one summer my nan offered to buy her a new one from Argos. She was worried about Nanny Beckett sitting at home doing nothing all day and not using her brain. At least the obsession with writing things down kept her active to an extent. My nan would visit her a few times a week, but now that the TV was broken Nanny Beckett let the world pass her by.

But not having a TV took a weight off Nanny Beckett's shoulders; if the information was out of sight, her problems were out of mind. Huge world events would take place and Nanny Beckett would have no idea they'd happened because she refused to let my nan buy her a television.

When I got a new mobile phone at Christmas she refused to look at it, simply because she didn't have the energy to write down what it all meant.

'Don't show me it,' she begged. 'I'll only have to write it down.'

She became too scared to leave the house. She didn't want to converse with people, because it would mean having to remember everything they said. Any information or news she received was then relayed through my nan. We'd be sitting at home and she'd ring five, ten, fifteen times, just to make sure she'd got the stories correct, writing them down thoroughly as though she'd been there herself. We'd sigh, telling her yes, that was what X said, and, yes, that was what happened when we saw X out shopping. Anything to put her OCD at ease.

Seeing Nanny Beckett struggling made me see how serious OCD was and how much I didn't want to let my obsessions get the better of me. I feel thankful that I'm living in a time where more and more people are discussing mental health issues such as these, and where you're not put into a psychiatric hospital for suffering with severe anxiety. But sometimes, when the Brain Deviant rears its ugly head, you forget you're not the only one dealing with these issues. It's like your brain forgets how neurotic you acted before, and it feels new again. You slump back into a dark state of loneliness, wondering how you'll ever get out.

The problem was, Nanny Beckett could've got help, but she didn't want it. That's the thing with mental illness. You can't help people who don't want to help themselves.

One weekend, I was sitting in Nanny Beckett's living room, watching some mundane TV show as I did every Sunday to block out the sound of the hairdryer, when I overheard her chatting to my nan.

'Charlotte's put on a lot of weight, hasn't she?'

'Shh, Mum!'

'What? She has! She's put on a lot.'

'Be quiet,' my nan hissed, scared I'd overhear.

Weight gain? Huh? What was she on about? I mean, I *was* wearing an extra-large man's beige sweatshirt that covered every bit of my body – no wonder I looked bigger. I convinced myself I wasn't actually wearing such a hideous oversized sweatshirt to hide the body I'd gradually begun to hate. It was easier to blame Nanny Beckett's comments for how bad I felt, rather than admit to the self-loathing I'd been feeling for a while.

As we left, I couldn't look Nanny Beckett in the eye. I was embarrassed, but didn't want to bring it up with my nan, or let either of them think it had affected me.

When we got home, I went into the bathroom, locked the door, took my clothes off until they fell in a pile at my feet, and looked at myself in the mirror. Properly and intensely, this time – not through hurried and shy glances, as I would have usually.

It was true. My body *was* big. It was much bigger than any of the other girls' bodies in my class. I pressed into the flesh on either side of my ribs and my finger disappeared into my skin by a good inch or two. My tummy wobbled when I hit it. How had I not noticed this before? Was I blind as well as fat?!

I hit it again, and again, and again. It was like jelly on a plate, wibbly-wobbling away. It was disgusting. I couldn't believe I'd let myself get this way. I was a total mess.

I knew I had to change. And so that night I vowed to go on my very first diet.

I didn't want to seem ungrateful when my nan handed me my usual treats bag in the morning.

'Can I have a bit less in the bag today?' I asked, looking at the brightly coloured packets that seemed to glare back at me, begging me to eat them.

'Don't be so silly,' my nan said. 'You love your treats bag.'

Once I got to school, I opened the treats bag in secret and began to study the labels. It looked like a foreign language. What did these numbers mean? There were 250 'calories' in a packet of crisps; 220 in a chocolate bar. But there were none in a can of Diet Coke. Did that mean it was better for you? As I thought about it, my only reasoning was that worse foods had higher numbers. Diet Coke, for example, must be good, and chocolate must be bad.

'Here you go,' I said, giving my bag of food to the girls in my dorm. I watched as they fell over the treats like a pack of wild animals. My stomach may have been growling, but I liked the fact I'd managed to resist temptation. Finally, I felt in control.

Spring arrived, and so did swimming lessons. For someone who hated their body as much as I'd started to, these classes were complete hell.

For one, the swimming pool was outdoors, which meant you were constantly freezing, and it would frequently have a dead mouse/bird/rabbit (delete as applicable) floating on top of the water that would need fishing out. We had a strict gym teacher, Miss Miller, who'd yell at us from the sidelines if we complained about being cold, all while standing there in a warm tracksuit.

But the thing that put me off the most was having to wear a tight swimming costume next to a class of pretty, petite and skinny girls who I was much bigger than, both horizontally and vertically. While they looked like a bunch of delicate little swans paddling away in the pool, I looked like a blobby giant. I'd stand by the pool trying every which way to cover my tummy and thighs and other wobbly bits. I felt fat, and was utterly convinced the girls in my class viewed me that way, too.

The one way you could get out of swimming was if you were on your period. Being 'on' granted me the privilege of avoiding the cold water, and meant I could get out of showcasing my squishy body and erect nipples through my costume and having to shave my underarms and bikini line. So that's when I thought I'd use the thing that made me different to my advantage.

I would make my way over to Miss Miller every Tuesday, put my hand on my tummy and ask if I could go to the nurses' office for a hot-water bottle. She'd put a cross next to my name on the clipboard, then tell me to feel better soon.

Skiving off swimming was great. I'm convinced the nurses, who we had to call 'sisters', knew my game plan, but they didn't say anything. I became friendly with a few other girls in school, who I'm sure were often skiving off as well, and we'd hang out there chatting with hot-water bottles on our tummies. I'd sit in the sisters' office with Ribena and biscuits, watching crappy old videos on the VHS, before 'miraculously' getting better for my next lesson. It was great.

That was, of course, until Miss Miller cottoned on to what I'd been doing.

'You've been off swimming for four weeks in a row now,' she said, glancing down at her clipboard one Tuesday morning. 'Are you honestly trying to tell me you've had your period every single week this month?'

'I'm . . . very irregular,' I lied.

'Get changed into a costume and get in the pool, Charlotte.' Teachers only called me by my real name when I was in trouble, so I knew things were going to go slowly downhill from there.

'I don't have a costume,' I replied, which actually meant: 'It's currently scrunched away at the back of my cupboard.'

'Well, I suppose you're just going to have to wear a leftover one from lost property then,' Miss Miller said, smirking. 'Hurry up, please.'

The class watched from the side of the pool as Miss Miller led me to the changing rooms. She was clearly quite pleased with herself, loving the fact I was squirming, in a way I'm sure a serial killer gets off on, too.

'Here's a spare one,' she said, and flung me a navy-coloured costume that reeked of chlorine and possibly even body odour. (OK. I may have exaggerated that part.)

'I really don't want to wear somebody else's swimming costume,' I groaned, thinking of how the material would have clung to some other girl's bits. God knows how long it had been left in the changing room. It hadn't even been washed, for Christ's sake. Brain Deviant went into overdrive, yelling, '*PUBES! PUBES! PUBES!*' in my ear.

But Miss Miller wasn't having any of it. As I made my way back to the pool, with the repetitive and overpowering thoughts of having shared the material with somebody else's vagina, I just wished I could've saved myself the embarrassment of being paraded along the side of the pool in front of everyone and brought my costume with me. My thighs jiggled on the edge of the pool, and my cheeks flushed red with shame. My plan of hiding out of sight had instead made me a spectacle.

5

MILFS, MODELS AND MAGAZINES

Now fourteen, I was rather enjoying being the apple (*95 calories*) of my grandparents' eye when my parents announced they were moving back to England. While the idea of them moving back was nice, I couldn't help but feel a tiny bit annoyed about the changes that would be happening. I loved my mum and dad, obviously, but I also liked being the centre of attention with my nan and grandad.

Once my mum and dad moved back, life suddenly became very strict and boring. Gone were the days of being spoiled by my nan at weekends. Gone were meals out and takeaways. There were so many rules, rules, *rules* to abide by, and I felt like I was in trouble for absolutely everything. My dad began a new job in London, and would travel up to us every other weekend, so the most I spoke to him was down a phone.

The other annoying thing about my mum was that she was considered a MILF. Not to me, obviously (that would be weird), but she was, without question, a very attractive woman.

I didn't quite appreciate how good-looking she was until the girls in my class mentioned how 'fit' she was after she came to pick me up from school one day, which isn't really what you want to hear as a teenager, especially when you feel like you resemble a human slug. She was much younger than the other mums, with beautiful curly red hair and perfectly white straight teeth that lit up a room when she laughed – which is annoying, considering my teeth look like they've been put through a lawnmower.

She'd done a bit of modelling as a teenager, following in the footsteps of my nan, who had also won a few beauty contests in her youth. To top it off, my little sister was the picture of innocence – an angelic face and bright blonde bob, with a cute grin and little frame that everyone considered 'adorable'. Nobody said I was cute. Then again, why would they? I was a pain in the arse. It felt awfully unfair that I hadn't been blessed with the same looks as all these women in my family had.

'Is that your *mum*?!' people would say, and I would say, 'Yes, that is my mum.' 'But she looks so young!' they'd add, as though being youthful was some sort of an achievement, and I would smile through gritted teeth, saying, 'Yes, she had me at twenty-four.'

Mum was a size eight; I was bordering on a size twelve to fourteen. Her boobs were a pert and perfect C cup – I was lucky if I filled out a B.

I knew people questioned how someone as beautiful and as slim as my mum could possibly be related to someone like me. That's how I felt, too. On top of people calling my dad a DILF (yuck) or my sister 'cute', I couldn't have felt more unrelated to my family if I'd tried.

Since I'd been bullied in my last school, I had no confidence whatsoever. Nothing I did could bring the old me back or make me feel confident again, even though I'd formed a small group of friends by this point. I developed a stutter and, when speaking, would have to come up with another word in my head that didn't begin with the letters 'W', 'L', 'R' or 'K', so as not to make an idiot out of myself. My life was spent constantly second-guessing everything and wondering if I'd offended someone somehow – more unresolved anxiety.

I don't know why I thought everybody hated me. I was by no means 'cool', but I wasn't a total geek, either. But what was the point in making friends anyway? I'd only be taken out of this school in a couple of years' time. I didn't want to get hurt again.

As far as I was concerned, everybody in my class hated me. They surely must've viewed me in the same way my ex-classmates in Belgium did, and I couldn't blame them. I mean, what was there to like? I was still the class clown, but when I played up in class and made people laugh I assumed they were laughing *at* me, not *with* me. I believed I was worthless, and that I didn't belong anywhere.

Eventually, the paranoia I felt about people hating me became unbearable. The negative voices hissed and murmured in my head like snakes. Night-times made it worse: I'd go over and over images of girls huddling together and giggling about me behind my back. The Brain Deviant would whisper in my ear, telling me that people were gossiping about me and saying how much of a loser I was. I know people gossiped about me to an extent – we were teenage girls, after all. But all I was absolutely paranoid about was not being liked.

It's embarrassing for me to admit, but I would get the overwhelming urge to ask girls in my class if they liked me or not, with the same level of urgency I did when I had to pray to the invisible Brain Deviant for my sins, or when I had to obsessively wash my hands in case something bad happened.

'Do you like me?' I'd ask pleadingly, hoping desperately that they'd say they did. They'd be sympathetic the first few times I asked, nodding in agreement and saying 'Of course!' as though I was being silly, but once I'd asked them four or five times over a period of a week it understandably began to p*ss them off. Yet again, I knew I wasn't acting sane, but the urge to get their approval was like an itch I needed to scratch. The phrase 'Do you like me?' would spill out of my mouth in conversation, even if I didn't want it to.

I was in the canteen one lunchtime, heading over to my table, when a chorus of girls in my class called out to me:

'Charli, do you like me?'

'What about me, Charli? Do you like me?'

'What about *me*?!'

They burst into fits of giggles, and I was left clutching my plate with a very red face. Why, oh *why*, couldn't I make myself normal?!

I wished they knew I couldn't control the insecure words that spewed out of my mouth. I wished they could've understood the jumbled mess and unexplainable fear in my brain, or the feeling of nausea in my lower gut. Most of all, I wished they could've understood how truly desperate I was to be liked.

I didn't know why I was still at that school. I'd been excited about going to boarding school to begin with, but I always assumed I'd leave when my parents moved back. I'd even written them an angry letter saying how much I hated it and wanted to leave. Isn't that how you resolve things? By writing angry letters?!

But my mum and dad thought boarding school was a great way of keeping things in my life consistent, in a lifestyle where schools and houses weren't permanent. By the time they moved to England to be nearer to my school I was living in house number nine. And even though they thought they were doing their best, and even though I can see it from their point of view now, I just didn't view it that way at the time.

I received my first fashion magazine in something called the Birthday Sack, which was basically a pillowcase that your friends would take from dorm to dorm the night before your birthday, in which girls would gift you totally random and unnecessary things both you and, most importantly, *they* didn't need.

Among the array of toothbrushes, perfume samples and sweets that I'm sure had been lying at the bottom of someone's handbag, was a copy of *Elle*. Its edges were tatty, and it had clearly been read by a lot of people, but instantly I became hooked.

First off, it had Elvis's granddaughter on the cover, dressed in bright neon colours and pink-and-purple-striped socks with high heels. I'd never seen anyone look so beautiful or glamorous. Aside from once having Michael Jackson as a stepfather, I bet she didn't have any problems. Secondly, the articles in it seemed so grown-up and glamorous compared to the 'What does my discharge mean?' questionnaires in my teen magazines. I treasured that magazine like it was my most prized possession, reading it from cover to cover.

This magazine was my escape from boarding school. I dreamt I was in the shoes of the models who were shooting in exotic locations. I bet those girls weren't expected to play lacrosse on a rainy sports field, or made to wear leftover swimming costumes by their bitch of a PE teacher. Nah – their lives looked whimsical and perfect. If only I was a model . . .

Oh, who was I kidding? Like that would ever happen.

Still, it didn't mean I couldn't fantasize about becoming one – even if I looked nothing like a model. I dreamt of being on the pages, where some place, somewhere, some girl would want to look like me. But in order to become one I needed to become thinner.

That's what models were: thin. There were no Ashley Grahams lining the pages, and certainly no 'body positive' movements. Instagram didn't exist, so there were no models doing their own thing and modelling at the size they were meant to be. You were expected to hate your body – because, as all retailers know, getting women to hate their bodies sells more products.

The supermodels of the eighties, models like Naomi Campbell and Cindy Crawford, were, at this stage, probably considered 'fat'. Now every model you saw looked anorexically thin.

In fact, it seemed that every celebrity was size zero. Size zero was everywhere. Weekly gossip magazines would print hundreds of images of these thin women, parading them like their obvious mental illnesses were something to be gawped at. It was a very irresponsible thing to publish, especially for girls like me who were easily triggered and influenced by images like that, but you couldn't pick up a magazine without reading about it. Those images were hard to escape, and hard to steer your eyes away from.

I remember reading an article in one of these magazines, with a photo of a clearly anorexic celebrity next to it. The magazine had written '*HOW DOES SHE DO IT?*' at the top of the article, along with a step-by-step daily meal guide of what she probably ate. The total amounted to a mere 800 calories a day. I doubt you'd be able to print that in a magazine nowadays, but back then I remember cutting that segment out and keeping it in my purse like some sort of Holy Grail. Reading about size-zero models didn't deter me from eating disorders – it gave me the inspiration to look the same.

Now, perhaps you're someone who isn't easily influenced by reading that kind of thing, and can let these photos go through one ear and out the other, so to speak. But seeing that diet plan fuelled my already-distorted body image and gave me more of an incentive to achieve my size-zero goal. It was just the encouragement I needed.

People believed that size zero was a choice. Women 'chose' to look that way, didn't they? As it was a beauty ideal at the time, perhaps that's how it started for some women. Thin was fashionable. These women wanted to stay 'en vogue'. But while it may start off as a 'choice', when it's this drastic, it comes with consequences. There is only one way to become that thin, and that's by starving yourself.

If fashion wanted to shock, it did. It created millions of headlines and photo opportunities for brands everywhere. Some models I know from that time now recall being told to 'look anorexic, but not actually be anorexic'. So, if you were a model and wanted to book big jobs, that's what you did: diet until you looked excessively thin. Some models said they lived off apples and Diet Coke for years to keep the weight down and book jobs. Others injected heroin, took cocaine or ate balls of cotton to suppress their appetite. You could never look 'too thin'. One model even died coming off the catwalk due to starvation.

As seasons went on, the girls got thinner and thinner, before size double-zero became popular. And at that time millions of girls around the world who, like me, aspired to be models, assumed that having this body shape was necessary to be considered 'beautiful'. When skinny white women are the only women you see represented in the things you see and read, why wouldn't you believe that is the ideal?

Worse of all, size zero wasn't a trend. It lasted for years and years, was photographed for years and years and was written about for years and years. This body type would influence me as a teen and throughout my early twenties, and leave me with both physical and mental health problems.

It was a simple diet. That was all. Not even a diet, really – just choosing to lead a healthy lifestyle, choosing not to eat copious amounts of chocolate bars or junk. Cutting down on cans of Coke and lemonade. Not having double portions of everything. Being in control of what I put into my mouth, when I hadn't been able to stop myself from binge-eating before.

And it worked! The weight did come off – a healthy amount. I was by no means skinny, and I was still 'bigger' than most girls in my class, but I was slowly becoming 'normal' like the rest of them.

My new obsession was pulling my jumper up to my neck and seeing if I could see a bit of ribcage yet. The inches of fat that had previously covered my ribs seemed to have shrunk ever so slightly, as had the squishiness of my tummy. No one else seemed to notice my efforts, though. Although the scales were going down, no one mentioned that I'd lost weight, and this felt frustrating.

Limiting what I ate didn't make me feel any better about myself, but it did make me feel in control and gave me something to focus on other than homesickness and the constant paranoia and anxiety. Well, it wasn't like I had control in any other aspect of my life, was it? I felt trapped at a school I didn't like very much, on a campus in the Welsh countryside predominantly surrounded by sheep and rabbits with myxomatosis. Like most teenagers, I desperately wanted freedom.

So now, eating was my new obsession. Or rather, not eating. Every meal was a test of my willpower, and became an even bigger excuse to put myself down.

My control over food was drowning out my anxiety – and so was bad behaviour. I did have one best friend in school – Dave the Woman. Dave wasn't a man, obviously, but I do have a ton of fond memories of her, and she was great.

Dave the Woman came from a very wealthy family. Her mum was very beautiful and fashionable and let us get away with a lot, so going to her house was a lot of fun and a retreat away from the prison. The thing I loved most about Dave was that she was always up for a laugh, and humour-wise she was just as immature as I was. She also hated boarding school as much as I did, and so we'd lean on each other when times got hard.

I suppose you're wondering how Dave the Woman got gifted her name. Well, back in the days when YouTube was merely a twinkle in the internet's eye, Dave was given a camera you could record videos on. A few people had uploaded videos to YouTube, but it wasn't that popular. However, for two bored schoolgirls, it was very popular indeed.

After a series of in-jokes that were funny to nobody bar us, the character Dave the Woman was born. Dave wasn't a man or a woman, really – just a crazy person who wore a pink bobble hat, a beige sweater and who would go around the school doing random things, like making prank calls; hitting fire alarms and running away; hitting vending machines until packets of crisps fell out; ringing the school payphone and watching through the window as we told someone they were going to get murdered by a ghost; or pretending to 'tree watch' – i.e. sitting on a wall outside the dormitories and waiting to see if a tree moved or not. It was silly, but it took our minds off being homesick – and Dave and I were both incredibly homesick. Homesickness bonded us, but also got us into a lot of trouble.

Once our video compilation of Dave's adventures was complete, I'd sit on my laptop and edit them together before uploading them to YouTube. Famous YouTubers like Zoella certainly didn't exist back then, but I'd like to think that had I kept it up I'd probably be as good as her now (and maybe as rich).

But you know what? Dave the Woman's video took off. It began to get shared hundreds of times across a popular social media site for teens at the time called Bebo, which was like – in my humble opinion – a crap version of Facebook. Kids from schools across the county shared our video, and Dave the Woman became an internet sensation – well, at least among a few schools in the north.

The filming of Dave the Woman took up the majority of our spare time. People couldn't wait to see what 'adventures' Dave got up to next, like what would happen after we cling-filmed toilet bowls in the middle of the night. Even boys found it funny, which in hindsight isn't that surprising, considering our videos were very immature.

But then I had the grand idea to make *Dave the Woman: The Movie*. This was going to be our funniest video yet, and would help viewers understand the real Dave. I was the presenter, and we got another friend to film it.

During one scene, we wanted to artistically show the viewer that Dave had the mindset of a child. As if by magic, a group of ten-year-olds were coming out of their PE lesson. When the teacher's back was turned, we decided to get them involved.

'Would you like to be on TV?' I said, holding the camera in my hand. 'We're filming something for the BBC.'

'Yes! Yes! Yes!' they squealed.

'Great!' I said. 'When I put my thumb up, I need you to all wave your hands, OK?'

'OK!' they said enthusiastically.

'Three . . . two . . . one . . . *action*!' I said, and Dave jumped into the frame.

'These are my friends! They are all little children!' she yelled excitedly, and once I'd put my thumb up, the kids started waving.

'And . . . cut!' I yelled, which was handy, because the teacher had just walked back.

It was great footage. Once it had all been edited, it was uploaded to the internet and people went crazy for it. Dave would walk in the street and people would yell 'Dave!' like she was some sort of celebrity.

Meanwhile, some teacher at our school, who clearly had no life of her own, had set up a secret Bebo account to spy on what the girls were doing. No, I'm not joking. In fact, a lot of girls had been in trouble in school recently for posting things online, and none of us could work out who the snitch was. But because *Dave the Woman: The Movie* was going semi-viral, and because this teacher had no life, she'd spotted the video one evening. And rather than view it as the Oscar-worthy piece of artistry it was, she found a big issue with it – which may have been understandable.

Her daughter was one of the kids waving.

We were sitting in assembly one Friday morning when our headmaster made an announcement.

'It's come to my attention that some girls have been filming some incredibly offensive things and posting them on to the internet,' he said. 'I've been told by one member of staff that it's borderline pornographic.'

Everyone began whispering, wondering who he could be talking about. You see, we weren't the only girls filming videos and uploading them. Dave the Woman's internet success had encouraged other girls in our school to follow suit, and while their videos may not have been as deep and artistic it was still cool that our success was being used as inspiration.

It couldn't have been us – could it? I mean ... pornographic? What was he on about? Was Dave pretending to wank off a tube of chocolate 'pornographic'?

'We did film that lady in the nude,' Dave whispered next to me. Oh yes – the life-drawing model, who we'd filmed in the style of a David Attenborough documentary through the window of the art block.

'So I'm giving these girls the chance to bring themselves forward by the end of today,' the headmaster continued. 'And if they don't, there will be severe consequences.'

No one was going to hand themselves in if their videos hadn't been watched, were they? But that didn't mean we weren't sick with worry that it was us. We tried deleting the videos that break time, but YouTube had been banned that morning on the school's network (how convenient). Lauren the Goth, another close friend, rang her boyfriend to log on to our YouTube account and take it down.

We must've got away with it. Phew!

As if.

We'd just finished another mundane assembly on Monday morning when Dave, the videographer and I were tapped on the shoulder by the deputy head.

'You three – come with me. *Now*,' she said in a very menacing voice.

So I guess it was our videos then. She led us to the headmaster's office, which was occupied by a police officer. I wasn't an idiot – I knew the policeman was there as a scare tactic, and the whole thing felt like it had been massively blown out of proportion.

'Sir, I don't really get what the problem is,' I said.

'The problem? *THE PROBLEM?!*' he yelled. 'You are *CHILDREN* who uploaded videos of yourselves to the internet doing *OBSCENE* things!!!'

'Well . . . yes, but they weren't "obscene",' I said, trying to reason with him, as Dave and the videographer sat there quietly.

'I've heard they're *pornographic*!'

'I can tell you they *weren't*,' I said, beginning to get offended. After all, this was my directorial debut he was slagging off. 'I know we filmed a naked lady, which was out of order, but we can show you them if you want . . .'

'I've been told they're not appropriate for me to see!' he yelled. 'Do you think I want to be arrested?!'

As this was unfolding, PC Plod was taking notes in his notebook. Jesus Christ. You would've thought we'd filmed a murder.

'You hacked the school's network in order to upload it!' the headmaster kept yelling, which was admittedly kind of true. I was quite good at computer stuff, even if I did say so myself. 'Why would you even think making these videos was a good idea?!'

'It's had loads of hits,' I said.

The headmaster sighed and told Dave and the videographer they could leave. 'You,' he said, pointing his finger at me, 'can stay here.' Once they had left, he carried on. 'I blame you in all of this.'

I couldn't help but feel he was being incredibly unfair. The videos weren't all my fault. He always seemed to pick on me, like the time a group of us were yelling loudly during Christmas hymns and he told me off, not everyone else, or when a group of us decided to go trick-or-treating in the local village and scared some old lady.

He reeled all these stories off, as though he'd saved them up for an opportune moment. There was the time I'd convinced a friend to go to the local village pub with me one wintry Thursday evening, and when we opened the front door we came face-to-face with a table full of teachers. We were fourteen and dressed in school hoodies, so I don't know how we ever thought we'd get served, but there you go. The teachers were as shocked as we were, and we stared at each other for what felt like five minutes, before I slowly shut the door in their faces. By the time we ran back to school our housemistress was trying to de-ice her car in an attempt to rescue us. Can you *imagine* how much trouble she'd be in for not paying attention to two schoolgirls who were meant to be in her care?! Don't worry, she told us enough times in the half-hour she spent yelling at us afterwards.

Oh, and then there was the time me and a couple of friends broke into a dormitory at the nearby boys' boarding school one weekend and tried on one guy's clothes before being caught by a teacher. We'd lied and said we were his cousins, yet somehow it got relayed back to my housemistress, and we were put in detention again. Or the time we went down to the garage one evening and got into a fight with some local kids, and the caretaker drove through the field in a Range Rover to save us.

To be fair, there was a lot of instances. Perhaps I was starting to show a pattern of bad behaviour.

Once I'd been dismissed from his office, I joined Dave and the videographer in my housemistress's office where, would you believe, we had to write 'police statements' about the videos in total silence. Then the videographer turned to the housemistress.

'Umm . . . in one of the videos, Dave pretended to . . . to . . .'

'To what?'

'You know,' she said.

'No, I don't know.'

'Umm . . . you know . . .' She started to do hand movements. '*Masturbate.*'

Dave's head popped up from across the office.

'I just put "wank",' Dave said matter-of-factly.

Well, when my headmaster read '*Dave pretended to wank*' in front of the police officer, he went mental again. My mum got called into the staffroom, and he made some arsey comment about how I was 'lucky' to be at such a prestigious school, and if I wanted to stay I had to stop misbehaving. I secretly hoped something I did would get me expelled so that I could finally leave.

6

BOYS, BODY HAIR AND BULIMIA

Back when my big bushy eyebrows were considered the most unattractive quality in the world (oh, how times change), I one day decided to go to Boots and buy myself some hair-lightening cream – you know, the white burning cream women use to bleach their moustaches. I'd come up with an ingenious plan to bleach the in-between monobrow bit, so that it would save me time plucking.

I was sick of having to pluck the hairs from between my eyebrows like some sort of hairy monkey. None of the other girls in my class seemed to have to pluck theirs – their eyebrows were thin and perfectly shaped. Besides, what boy would fancy someone with caterpillars on their face? Women were expected to be smooth and hairless, weren't they?

I'd had comments from girls and boys about how bad my eyebrows were. One boy told me at a summer fete that he'd probably fancy me if they weren't so big, and I was mortified.

Girls in my class would offer to pluck my eyebrows for me as though they were doing me a favour. Hell, even Dave the Woman's mum asked me if she could pluck them one weekend. No wonder I was paranoid! When I'd give in and become their test guinea pig, anxiously sitting on the edge of my bed clutching a mirror, they'd pluck them so thin that I'd always end up looking surprised, and not in a good way. Even though thin eyebrows didn't suit me in the slightest, I was pretty sure that by looking like other girls I was going to look as nice as they did, too. (I didn't.)

I truly took to heart what other people thought about me – especially boys. I thought their views on how my body looked were more important that my own. But the problem with boys nowadays is that they grow up seeing totally unrealistic images of women, and therefore assume girls are perfectly hairless and smooth, a bit like those weird-looking Sphynx cats, or Phil Mitchell. The idea that women may have, God forbid, *body hair* comes as a real shock to some boys – and, sometimes, even to some girls. That's because they listen to what boys have to say about their bodies, feeling like some kind of monster because their pubes don't grow out like a perfectly rectangular landing strip, or because they have (shock horror!) hair on their underarms.

I wish I could shake teenage Charli and say: 'You are not a Sphynx cat. You are not Phil Mitchell. Just like you have eyebrows, you also have pubes, and the reason you have hair in those places is because *you're human*. Men aren't pressured to wax or tweeze or to get rid of their body hair, even when they resemble a human rug, so why the hell should you?'

Anyway, back to eyebrows. I probably don't need to tell you that putting any form of bleach near your eyes is a stupid idea, but I was stupid, and a bit lazy, and I certainly didn't like the instructions telling me what to do.

'You all right in there?' my nan yelled, knocking on the bathroom door.

'YES! Don't come in!'

Using the miniature spoon, I smothered the bleach on to the monobrow bit, trying desperately hard not to breathe in the smell, which was overwhelmingly acidic. But because the bathroom light was so unflattering and dim, I accidentally got it on my eyebrow itself. I'm sure you don't need to be a hair colourist to understand that because my eyebrows are so dark and coarse, it turned my left eyebrow various shades of orange. It took at least three weeks to grow out properly.

When that didn't work, and once the orange had eventually faded, I began getting my eyebrows waxed instead. Although I assume the intense smell of incense in the beauticians was meant to make me feel calm, that soon went when Susan the beautician waxed my face. It bloody hurt. Still, I kept going every two weeks to keep my eyebrows topped up and to fit in with the other girls in my class. Whenever she'd hand me the mirror afterwards to admire her grand masterpiece, I'd smile through gritted teeth and tell her how great it looked, despite resembling *The Scream*.

The reason I stopped going in the end wasn't necessarily because thin eyebrows didn't suit me, but because after at least three sessions I'd leave her salon holding a bloody tissue to my eyebrows where she'd ripped my actual skin off. Pain, I soon learnt, does not equal beauty.

By this stage, I was sixteen. There was no part of my body that society wasn't telling me to hate, and I was miserable. And as though despising myself wasn't sh*t enough, it's time to introduce you to bad boyfriend number one.

It's probably time to point out that throughout my life I have often been known to date losers. I'm aware that makes me sound like I'm up myself, or that I look down my nose at people, but hear me out. I have a tendency to date boys who treat me badly, because I often feel it's all I deserve. When you're an unhappy person you don't feel you deserve people being nice to you.

They're the men who put you down, because it's easier for them to project their own insecurities on to you than to deal with their own. They are the men your mothers warned you about and who your dads want to punch in the face, but whose faults you like to shove under the carpet because one day 'they'll change'.

These boys don't start off like that, of course. At first, you are entranced by their charms. They're exciting. They live freely. They're fun and make you laugh. You think they're so wonderful that you fail to see the negatives. And when I go through low or anxious periods, I tend to be drawn to them more than ever.

Mark was a tall, dark, drop-dead handsome hunk of a man (well, boy) who would become my first male obsession.

He lived in Cheshire in the house next door to Dave the Woman, a two-hour drive away from our school, and would frequently hang around with Dave and her sister at weekends. I first met him at Dave the Woman's annual Halloween party, when I was dressed as a 'sexy bunny' (i.e. a tight grey dress with pink-and-white-foam bunny ears from Claire's Accessories. Spooky), and once we'd broken the ice over bottles of blue WKD I began noticing that he'd deliberately try to hang around me at any opportune moment. And yet whenever I'd try to strike up a grown-up conversation with him, he'd stumble over his words and become shy, his cheeks blushing bright pink.

Mark was incredibly handsome, with dark brown hair, olive skin, chocolatey brown eyes and a very dashing smile. I'd never seen a boy as good-looking as him before, let alone spoken to one. I couldn't understand how someone as handsome as him could be so shy. He'd hide behind his emo fringe, occasionally looking down at the floor if we made eye contact. Weirdly, he seemed to find everything I said hilarious, laughing loudly and hysterically at things that weren't even meant to be funny (but it did wonders for my ego).

Someone as gorgeous as Mark couldn't fancy me ... could he? Me? I mean, what did I possibly have to offer a man? I had over-plucked eyebrows that resembled sperm and a moon of a head. Nah, of course he couldn't have done. Who was I kidding?

But the following day, after the Halloween party, Mark popped round to spend time with us before my nan came to pick me up. He seemed a bit more confident that day, showing off and making jokes while Dave's mum grilled burgers on the barbecue. There was definitely a bit of chemistry between us, even if I couldn't pinpoint what that feeling was yet.

Not long after, Mark added me on MSN, an online instant messaging site that was basically WhatsApp before WhatsApp. We began chatting, and I could have sworn he was flirting with me, but I wasn't sure. Besides, Dave the Woman had a crush on him, so I couldn't go there.

That didn't mean I couldn't ogle him from afar, though. Soon, I'd boycotted going to my nan's at weekends to spend time at Dave's house, where the three of us would wander round town together, hang out in the garden or watch films. It was perfectly innocent, despite the fact I desperately wanted to eat his face.

One Saturday evening, the three of us had gone to Blockbusters to rent a movie. (I know, imagine the days when you had to get into a car and drive to a shop to rent a movie, rather than streaming it online?!) Although I didn't particularly want to watch a scary film, I thought it'd be a perfect opportunity to snuggle up next to Mark and pretend to be 'frightened'.

Mark sat between me and Dave with the popcorn perched on his lap, and despite the gore, blood and screams on the screen my heart began beating faster.

Then, underneath the blanket, Mark squeezed my hand. I froze.

WHAT. WAS. HAPPENING?

'I'm just going to get some more popcorn,' Dave announced. 'Anyone want a drink?'

Mark and I smiled at her. 'No!' we said at the same time in high-pitched voices, and once the door shut we looked at each other.

Before you knew it, I found myself having my first proper grown-up kiss. It wasn't like my first teenage kiss, which was at an underage disco with a boy called Charlie who seemed to have a slug for a tongue. This was great. Mark was a hundred-per-cent-certified Sex God. In fact, it was so great that we didn't hear Dave walk back into the living room . . .

'WHAT THE HELL IS GOING ON?!' Dave yelled, making us jump apart.

'Erm, well . . .' I stuttered. I had forgotten that Dave fancied Mark as much as I did. She stormed out of the room, Mark left (after kissing me goodbye, of course), and Dave and I had a huge argument about it all night.

But that was it. I was smitten. Once Dave and I had stopped rowing, Mark and I were an actual couple, which was made official over MSN. I still failed to believe that someone as fit as Mark was *my* boyfriend, but somehow life was finally looking up.

From then on, most of my weekends were spent with Dave the Woman and Mark. Boarding school suddenly felt bearable, because it meant I had him to look forward to at weekends, and I would eagerly cross off the days on my calendar until I saw him. I was absolutely obsessed with him, stalking his Facebook and MySpace accounts to see what he was up to, or just to gawp at his model-esque selfies. I doodled his name across my diaries and notebooks. We chatted during the day via text and every night online, making the most mundane of topics like school or family feel like the most exciting things in the world. I clung on to every word Mark said like glue, thinking he could do no wrong. We were totally inseparable for people who went to two different schools in two different counties and who only saw each other at weekends.

I'm aware I'm making Mark out to be the Sex God of the North. Not that I'd know – we never had sex. Our relationship was perfectly innocent and sweet, full of holding hands and trips to the cinema. My dad did warn me that boys of that age only wanted 'one thing', but I couldn't imagine Mark – a sixteen-year-old boy who still had a teddy bear named Gregory in his bed – being remotely interested in sex. He'd certainly never mentioned any interest in it to me. In fact, the closest we ever got to it was getting a bit overexcited in a photo booth in Boots one afternoon and scaring some innocent old lady who pulled open the curtain half to death. (Needless to say, she went elsewhere to get her passport photos taken.)

Although I was supposed to be studying for my GCSEs, the only thing I wanted to study was Mark's gorgeous face. A lot of the time we had to see each other at Dave's, but there's only so many times you can snog the boy you both fancy in front of your best mate without her getting fed up, so we began seeing each other alone in Manchester instead, despite the fact it would take me over two hours to travel there on the train each time. I couldn't wait for the summer holidays to come, when I hoped we could see each other every day.

'Why do you always have to go on the train to where Mark is when you meet up?' my mum asked me one afternoon.

'What do you mean?' I snapped. I couldn't believe she had the audacity to say such a thing. HELLO, MOTHER, IT'S CALLED BEING IN A RELATIONSHIP. LOOK IT UP.

'Mark never meets you halfway,' she said. 'It takes you two and a half hours to travel up there on the train every Saturday. You're always having to spend your money on trains to Manchester, but he never seems to want to meet you in the middle.'

I knew my mum had a point. My bank balance was slowly dwindling. But I was also a moody teenager who had far more knowledge about boys after my sixteen years on the planet than she did after her forty. Who the hell did she think she was?

'Just leave it,' I said, and stormed off to my room (probably. I did that a lot).

That night, though, I thought about what my mum had said. It was true – Mark always had an excuse as to why he couldn't come on a train and visit me. But I was so thrilled to have a boyfriend, so excited to have such a *handsome* boyfriend, that I would've done anything to keep him happy.

I knew I was going to screw it up.

The Brain Deviant kept telling me I didn't deserve Mark – that I was ugly and fat and a waste of space, and that soon enough he'd see it for himself. Very soon, the Brain Deviant told me, Mark would wake up and realize what kind of troll he was with. It was just a matter of time before he came to his senses.

Over time, my anxiety and low self-esteem became so overwhelming that something very strange indeed began happening.

BLEURGHHHHHH!!

Yes, that's right. I would actually vomit in this handsome boy's presence whenever I saw him.

Every.

Single.

Time.

One day, Dave the Woman and I decided to accompany Mark and his best mate, George, to Manchester for a day of shopping. Mark idolized George, who was funny, witty, popular and handsome in his own way. (Looking back, he would have made a far better boyfriend than Mark ever did, but that's hindsight for you.) The boys decided we should all get kebabs for lunch, and, when impressing a boy, having drabs of greyish-brown meat slobbering out of your mouth isn't exactly sexy. But eager to please Mark and to be seen as 'one of the boys', I went along with their lunch of choice.

Food and I had a pretty strange relationship at that time. I was skipping most meals, focusing only on making myself beautiful for Mark. I wasn't used to eating – not even on my own. Let alone in front of my *boyfriend*.

I could practically see the calories sweating off the doner meat as it spun round on the rack. I could picture the germs that I imagined were covering the floor and tables of the gross establishment we'd stepped into. As I hesitantly took a bite into the kebab, I suddenly felt a wave of nausea.

'Oh God.'

'What?' Dave whispered.

'I'm gonna be sick,' I said, covering my mouth with my hand, and ran to the toilet, which looked even more germ-riddled. My anxiety was in overdrive as I began wondering what a joke Mark and George must've thought I was.

Germs. Calories. Fat. Germs. Calories. Fat. The images spun round my head like a merry-go-round.

Once I'd been sick, my face red from the exertion of vomiting, not to mention from embarrassment, I made my way back to the table.

'Are you OK?' Mark asked, and I hesitated, paranoid he'd still be able to smell the sick on me.

'I'm great!' I lied, and eased away from him slightly, trying to avoid staring at any form of food whatsoever. It was my fault for being so weak as to eat in front of him.

After that, throwing up in front of Mark became a regular occurrence. We'd be holding hands through the high street and I'd have to practically hold my sick in. We'd be watching a film at Dave's and I'd have to run to the toilet to throw up. One afternoon, George, Mark and I went to the woods, and I threw up in a pile of leaves (I still hope I didn't puke on a hedgehog in the process). We were once at George's house, sitting at the dinner table with his parents, who'd cooked us a delicious dinner, and I was seconds away from throwing up in the plate of chilli.

I wasn't being sick because Mark repulsed me in any way, because he didn't. He was *dreamy*. It was simply because I was so overwhelmed that someone as good-looking and cool as Mark could ever possibly want me as his girlfriend; my brain couldn't compute it. I genuinely believed I didn't deserve someone as perfect as him, or that other girls would question what he was doing with someone as uncool as me. I was not in peak physical condition anyway, because I was constantly starving.

I was so paranoid about coming across weird or doing something embarrassing in front of him that I couldn't just enjoy the moment or be myself. Which is *mental*, because throwing up in front of the boy you think you love is far from normal to say the least. And gradually I began changing who I was in order to make him like me more.

On the days I was at school and didn't see Mark, I began restricting what I ate even more. I wanted him to see a difference in the fat slob he'd met at the beginning of our relationship. I wanted him to see a difference in me every time.

Losing weight was soon the most important aspect of my life, to the extent that it almost replaced daydreaming about Mark. And soon I had my first goal to look my best for: Dave the Woman's Super Sweet Sixteenth.

Dave's mum was the glamorous mum of our year, and was allowing us to have actual *alcohol* at her daughter's party –

which, to any teenager, made her a very cool mum indeed. About twenty girls in our class were invited, but there was one problem.

'We can't have a party without boys, Dave,' I said.

Dave knew I was right. So she texted Mark, asking if he could bring a bunch of his friends along, to which he happily agreed. The news of this thrilled a bunch of schoolgirls. I was just excited by the fact that it would be my and Mark's first party as a couple. Him introducing me to his friends, and vice versa, was a sign we were *official*-official.

Although Dave's party soon became the topic of conversation during school break times, some mums in the class weren't happy about this party at all. If I'd ever thought my mum treated me like a baby, these mums made mine look like the chief of a free-love hippy commune.

'There will be boys/alcohol/a hot tub there?!' one particularly uptight parent rang to ask Dave's mum, despite the fact we were now *sixteen* and incredibly grown-up, thanks very much.

After Dave's mum managed to convince the Uptight Mum that no, her daughter would not be left alone with (shock horror!) a real-life boy, they came to the conclusion that her daughter was allowed to stay for a couple of hours, then she and a few of her friends would be picked up and taken home early.

Still, I wasn't going to allow the Uptight Mum's paranoia to ruin my evening.

'You've lost a lot of weight, Charli,' Dave's mum said, putting her arm round my shoulder, and I felt a rush of pride and excitement fill my veins. It was the first time anyone had noticed what I'd done, and it meant whatever I was doing was working. If she noticed, Mark must have noticed, too.

Mark arrived with three of his friends to begin with – George, Harry and Joe. George hated Joe. Joe was an emo, and brought along his girlfriend, Sarah, who was rather clingy and annoying, and George hated her, too. George hated everyone, actually, and was too cool for the lot of them. Harry was the son of a vicar, but couldn't have been less religious.

'Mark's told me so much about you,' Sarah squealed. 'I just knew we'd be friends! You are beautiful!'

To someone who'd never felt beautiful in her entire teenage life, Sarah's kind words comforted me slightly. But what made me feel even more special was when Mark squeezed my shoulders, letting her know I was with him.

'She's the most beautiful girl in the *world*,' he said, kissing me on the forehead, and I fell in love with him just a little bit more.

I wore his hoodie that night – a sign to any teenage girl that I was a hundred-per-cent his girlfriend. Before long, the party was in full swing. The birthday girl was drunk, everyone in the hot tub was either plastered or getting off with each other, someone was trying to pull Dave's mum, and Sarah kept hanging around me like a fly.

While my memory from then on is a bit hazy, all I know is that the Uptight Mum came to pick a group of tipsy girls up from the party just as it got good, and then me, Sarah,

Joe, George, Mark and a few other nameless faces were drinking in a zipped-up tent together in the garden.

'Get off with each other!' Mark said to me and Sarah while clutching a can of Stella. While I can say Sarah was definitely not my type, I wanted to please Mark, so I kissed her in an attempt to impress him.

Unlike when Katy Perry kissed a girl, I wasn't too sure I liked it. It wasn't because she was a girl, necessarily, but because (1) Sarah wasn't a good kisser, (2) she was actually quite irritating, and (3) having a bunch of male eyes gawping at us over cans of warm beer wasn't exactly a turn-on.

'*Gross!*' Mark yelled afterwards, even though he was the one who had encouraged it. God, he was charming.

'That was great,' Sarah said, and I smiled weakly, trying not to hurt her feelings.

'I need to chat to Charli alone for a minute,' Mark said, giving Joe, Sarah and the others a knowing look.

'Er . . . oh, yeah!' Joe said. 'Come on, guys, let's get some more drinks.'

Everyone left the tent suddenly, and I eventually realized through my tipsy state that Mark and I were alone.

After kissing for a few seconds, it became quite clear there and then what Mark wanted. And although I'd obviously thought about sex (hello, I was a sixteen-year-old girl) I was absolutely certain that losing my virginity in a tent that reeked of booze, and suspiciously like urine, was *not* what I wanted.

'No, Mark,' I said, pulling away.

'Oh, come on,' he said, starting to unzip my (well, his) hoodie from off my shoulders.

'I said no,' I repeated, pushing him away. Why wasn't he listening?

Mark sighed loudly, like I was the world's biggest let-down, and threw himself back down in the tent.

'Oh, whatever,' he said, and made some comment about how I was frigid.

'You're drunk,' I said.

'Yeah, yeah,' he said, waving me away.

I hated feeling like I'd done something wrong, and I had a real guilt complex about letting people down. But I got out of the tent, wished Mark goodnight without really meaning it, and went into Dave's house.

'Are you OK?' Dave asked once I got inside.

'Yeah, of course,' I lied. 'Come on, let's go to bed.'

To say I felt guilty for not having sex with Mark was an understatement. He made me feel terrible for not having done so.

You can imagine what this did for my self-esteem. You can also imagine what this then did for my anxiety. I believed that because he was acting off with me, that somehow made me less of a person. Once the excitement from Dave's party had calmed down and life got back to normal, something odd began happening to Mark.

You see, as time went on, and I fell deeper and deeper head-over-heels in love with him, Mark began to realize how good-looking he actually was. And, over time, something else became apparent:

Mark became a bit of a dick.

Now, realizing you're a good-looking bloke isn't the problem. It's when you think you can have your cake and eat it that it becomes a problem, or when you think your looks give you the right to behave or treat people in whichever way you want. (Note: they don't.) Mark revelled in the fact that girls practically threw themselves at his feet, and that boys wished they could look like him. If I didn't want to have sex with him, he certainly let me know there were plenty of girls who did. And it was during this time that he quite clearly latched on to my insecurities, and decided to put me down whenever he could.

It started off as an eye-roll here and there in front of his friends. They'd laugh at something I'd say and he'd tut and make out I was a nuisance, making me anxious again. It didn't matter that other people thought I was cool. The only person I wanted to impress was Mark.

We'd go shopping and girls would do double takes at him down the high street . . . and he'd then do double takes back. He'd tell me about a girl he knew, Jennifer, who allegedly had the world's best figure, and who all the boys fancied. He played on my insecurities, getting off on the fact he was knocking me down.

As a result, I started to overcompensate by starving myself more. He must've thought I was so gross with my flat chest and fat thighs, mustn't he? Maybe if I lost just a bit more weight, he'd view me like Jennifer. Maybe if I did it a bit quicker, he'd like me more.

I can't remember the first time I deliberately made myself sick, which I think goes to show how out of control I was. If I remembered the first time I made myself sick, it would've meant I was in control of my actions, when I can categorically say I was not.

I'd done it a few times a couple of years prior, around the ages of thirteen or fourteen, but it hadn't become a regular occurrence. I hadn't made a big deal of it at the time – it was just something I'd done. Weird, right? In fact, back then I didn't even know there was a word for my now biggest secret: bulimia.

I knew bulimia was when people deliberately made themselves sick. But *other* people suffered from bulimia, not me. I refused to admit I was as mental as they were. I wasn't crazy! I just liked getting rid of stress from time to time. What was wrong with that? It was a secret I kept between me and me only. If it wasn't hurting anyone, why did it need to be anybody else's business?

Despite the vile taste and texture in my mouth, all I recall is the overwhelming sense of relief – a feeling that nothing could get to me any more, that the calories I'd eaten no longer counted. I'm not saying Mark made me bulimic, because of course he didn't. He just added to the list of worries that were already ingrained in me, like not feeling wanted or loved, or not feeling like I was doing well in school. It was the final trigger I needed to send me over the edge. The catty comments, the self-loathing, the stress from exams, the insecurities I felt about Mark . . . it all disappeared in an instant.

I get why people find bulimia difficult to stomach (excuse the pun). Why would someone want to purposefully stick their fingers down their throat and make themselves vomit? Being sick isn't exactly pleasant, is it?

The truth is, there are lots of reasons. Yes, weight loss is of course a motivation, but the weird thing about bulimia is that you don't actually lose that much weight – if any – from throwing up. It's mainly water weight. Just as there are girls at a size eight who do it, there are girls who are size eighteen who do it. Bulimia doesn't discriminate. The underlying factor is that it's a stress reliever, and everyone, regardless of shape or size, wants to rid stress.

Now, I know I would've been better squeezing a stress ball or playing with a fidget spinner, but when you're in the midst of an eating disorder you're far from rational. You need to get rid of this angst and pressure as quickly as possible. All I can tell you is that once I'd been sick it felt like a weight had been lifted from within me. Well, obviously *some* weight had been lifted – heavy, thick, gross, lumpy, sour yellow and beige vomit, to be precise – but it was so much more than that. It was an invisible feeling of anguish that no one else quite understood, bar me.

My anxiety fuelled my bulimia. The Brain Deviant would tell me I was worthless, fat and gross, that it wasn't surprising everyone in school hated me or thought I was ugly. It was all my fault. It didn't take a lot to make myself sick. It could be homesickness, or an argument with my family, or the stress of not being able to finish an assignment. I didn't even need to be full to throw up.

Sometimes I'd binge and binge on food until I physically couldn't eat any more – crisps, cake, biscuits, bread – the delicious carby things that fill you up and give you the most energy. Then, when I was sure nobody was around, I'd down a ton of water to help the sick leave my body quicker, go to the toilets and throw it all up, fighting the sour and bitter taste in my mouth.

Once I'd made myself sick as much as I wanted or needed, I felt like I could see clearly again – that the foggy mist inside my head had cleared. Only then could I get on with the rest of my day and face problems head on. But that's the problem: it didn't solve anything.

In my experience, bulimia is an addiction. Once I'd done it and seen the stress disappearing in front of me, I somehow felt 'pure' again. Of course that feeling didn't last for very long. Most of what I experienced afterwards is the result of having physically worn my body out. Once I'd been sick so much that my body only produced bile, and I'd managed to calm my anxiety down a bit and recover slightly, I still hated myself. I became annoyed at my body for no longer being able to vomit properly. I was annoyed at myself for being a weak, pathetic person who couldn't eat food normally. *If you didn't binge eat, you wouldn't have to make yourself sick, would you?*

But I could no longer eat a normal amount of food like a normal person. It was everything in sight, or nothing at all.

Deep down, bulimia fed my obsessive and addictive behaviour – and rather than taking the time to calm myself down in a way that didn't harm myself, I'd do anything I could to rid myself of the anxiety quickly.

Whenever I got stressed again – which was inevitable, because, hey, that's life – I started getting the urge to throw up. Stress can come from many different places: pressure from exams, from parents, from not being able to digest a nasty comment or two, for hating your body or punishing yourself for eating too much. The reasons are unique to everyone who has it, and I'm just speaking for myself. Soon that familiar 'itch' would wash over me again, and I just NEEDED to get rid of it. I'd begin to feel sweaty, wondering how I could sneak out and throw up without people noticing. The last thing I wanted to do was get caught, because that would mean my secret would be out.

I have made myself sick in lots of different places in my life. I've done it in public toilets while out shopping, while my mum is blissfully unaware, flicking through the sales rack in a shop nearby. I've done it on holiday, while everyone is having fun by the pool. I've done it on a plane, and, no, I don't mean the Mile High Club. I've done it through critical episodes of *EastEnders* while my family is all together downstairs. I've done it on numerous birthdays and Christmases, throwing up delicious home-cooked food because I was too anxious about not knowing the exact calorie content, or because I was oversensitive to something a relative said. There should be a worldwide map with pins of places I've vomited in, including high above the Mediterranean Sea.

It was crazy, but it made sense to me at the time. And now I had another reason to be thin. I had a boyfriend, and a very good-looking one, to say the least. On the internet, I'd seen photos of the girls he hung around with and the competition I faced. If I wanted to keep him interested now that I'd turned down his offer of sex, I'd need to become thinner and thinner, until I was delicate and elegant – like the girls in the magazines, with their perfect relationships.

7

DAVE'S RAVE

I was sixteen, and utterly obsessed with being thin to the point of being considered desperately ill.

I was frequently staying with my dad at his flat in London at weekends, the umpteenth place he was now living, when model scouts began approaching me in the street. They'd hang around popular teenage places like Camden or Topshop on Oxford Street, hoping to find the next supermodel, and you'd occasionally watch eager mothers parade their daughters up and down in the hope they'd get spotted, too. But in my case, rather than getting signed, which is what you'd *assume* would happen if you were scouted a few times, it was always a case of never quite being good enough for agencies.

Getting scouted was a repetitive cycle. An agent would enthusiastically approach me in the street. They'd tell me how wonderful I looked. They'd hand me a business card. I'd be high on cloud nine. I'd gear myself up for days and go to the agency, full of high hopes and full-blown anxiety, starving myself even more ferociously for days in advance, wondering if this was my lucky break, and praying that it was. They'd *ooh* and *aah* for a bit, then would break the news that I'd be 'perfect' if it wasn't for my hips or my height or whatever other reason. They'd tell me to lose weight, and to come back when I'd lost it.

Umm, HELLO?!?! *They* had approached *me*. And after reeling me in, the answer was always the same – lose weight or your dreams won't come true. Looking back, I still can't believe that was even legal.

I wasn't fat, although at the time I thought I was far from skinny. I was tall by everyday standards, but at 5 foot 8 inches tall, I also didn't meet the standard model height criteria. I just didn't seem to fit in model-wise: a misfit, as it were. Being me wasn't good enough.

Rather than being supportive of me modelling, Mark seemed . . . well . . . *irritated* whenever I mentioned being scouted. His friends would say how cool it was, but he'd sit there rolling his eyes. He could've easily been a model – he was so handsome, and looks-wise I didn't compete with him in the slightest. But in a weird way it was like he hated me getting any form of attention.

Modelling was seemingly becoming more and more unlikely, though that didn't mean I didn't continue to dream about it, or attempt to reach my goals. Needless to say, at this time, my eating disorder was at an all-time high. It was the biggest part of my life, and dictated every minute of every day. Every decision was based on whether I'd have to eat: obsessively counting calories, jealously comparing myself to every girl I met. My obsession with modelling validated this behaviour.

Maybe if I kept losing weight I would get signed, and happiness would finally be in reach. I hadn't felt happy since the first time I compared my size to the other girls in the Angelz back when I was prepubescent. In my mind, the two were connected forever. As far as I was concerned, 'happiness' meant being 'thin', and being thin was achieved by watching EVERYTHING you ate.

It was also around this time that the career questions began. Everybody seemed to know what they wanted to do with their lives. One girl knew she was going to be a ballerina. Two girls knew they wanted to be vets. Dave the Woman wanted to get into childcare. And I didn't have a bloody clue.

Nothing stood out to me, unless you counted modelling as a career prospect (which it isn't, by the way). Any other jobs I liked the sound of were considered 'fantasy' by my parents, like working in television. Besides, this was at a time when EVERYONE and their dog (probably) went and got a university degree. If you didn't study something, you were considered a failure. And the last thing I wanted was to feel like I was letting people down again.

I had a truly amazing careers adviser who I went to visit at least three times a week, in the hope that she could spark a realistic interest for me. In fact, she encouraged me to become a model, after I'd told her I was interested in working in television.

'Have you thought about modelling?' she asked. 'You could do it. You should send your photos off to different agencies. A lot of people get into TV after being models.' She printed out a list of the country's best agencies for me, and I told her I'd submit my pictures.

I know that makes her sound a bit dodgy, but she was sound. Unlike a lot of adults, she took our career prospects seriously and told us not to listen to parents who had their own ideas of what their children should become.

'You don't want to wake up in thirty years' time having followed somebody else's dream,' she said, and this advice is so true. Your decisions may not please certain people at the time, but you're not put on this planet to please other people. Unless you're hurting someone, why shouldn't you go out and achieve your dreams?

On top of this stress, my dad then announced he had to go for a nine-month tour. In case you were wondering, that's not like a band tour, where musicians get drunk on a tour bus and have a bunch of groupies following them around. The military isn't exactly Thorpe Park and my dad's life was at risk from the second he went. I couldn't understand why he had to do this.

This tour wasn't the longest he'd been away from home – one year, he spent the entire twelve months away, and on Christmas Day we spoke to him over Skype. But was money worth this way of life? Nine months was another awfully long time without seeing him. This meant more anxiety for me, wondering if I'd ever see my dad alive again. Combined with the fact that I was physically weaker than I'd ever been, operating on barely any calories per day, I was a mess.

On the day before he was due to leave, my dad offered to take me for a driving lesson.

'I really can't drive today,' I said. While I may not have been shaking with nerves, my insides were wobbling like jelly. Nothing was making sense, and hadn't done for days, like I was having some sort of out-of-body experience.

'No, come on,' my dad said.

Reluctantly, I got into the driver's seat and began driving into town.

'Please can I stop?' I said nervously, dreading a roundabout ahead.

'You've got this!' he said. 'Come on!'

I was about to drive round the roundabout when my mind turned to mush. I accidentally put my foot down on the accelerator rather than the brake. My dad tried grabbing the steering wheel, but I shot across the roundabout and straight into a brick wall, hitting an ancient lead drainpipe. The car was completely screwed from the outside, the blue paint smeared across the brickwork.

'Oh, bother!' my dad said.

Just kidding.

'F*CK!!!' he yelled in the middle of the street. 'F*CK!!! F*CK!!! *F*CCCCKKKKK!!!*'

A crashed car and a bill for a broken wall was the last thing he needed the day before he left. But it also showed how bad my anxiety had become. I was an absolute nervous wreck. If I didn't feel like a freak before, I certainly did now.

When it came to losing weight, I did everything and anything I could to help lose it. Nothing – and I mean *nothing* – was off limits when it came to accomplishing my goal weight. You name it, I tried it. Whether it was legal or not didn't matter. I was willing to risk everything, including my health and sanity, to be thin.

Eating disorders are a Brain Deviant's dream. It gives you something for your OCD to cling on to and to obsess over (like how ugly you are, how unpopular you are, how many calories are in the food you're eating, getting down to an 'ideal' number on a scale, etc.), as well as feeding your anxiety – making your weight seem like the be-all and end-all of the world. It makes you believe that if you're thinner you'll have more friends, a boyfriend, that you'll be successful and in control of your life, or that you'll be prettier.

As far as I was concerned, being thin meant I would be liked by the girls in my class. It would mean I was paid attention. It would mean boys (i.e. Mark) would take an avid interest in me. Most of all, though, it would mean I was beautiful and 'model material' . . . and who wouldn't want that? My life's happiness boiled down to numbers on a scale, and only I had the power to achieve that.

In reality, my eating disorders did none of these things. They made me unsociable, because I was too afraid to go to a party and give in to temptation where food or alcohol was involved. I'd rather spend my time burning calories in a gym than hanging around in a common room watching TV with my friends. I began to get attention, but not in a good way: people thought I was acting erratically, but they didn't know how to deal with it, and so opted to brush the situation under the carpet.

I'd stand for hours looking at myself in the mirror, putting myself down. I often wonder how I'd be now if I'd spent that time telling myself how wonderful I was instead. '*You're disgusting*,' I'd tell myself. '*No wonder you don't have a boyfriend. Look at you. You make me sick.*'

I'd clutch at any fat I could find, desperately wishing it would shrink or disappear. I'd cry over cellulite, wondering why I seemed to be the only girl in my class with it. Even though I knew I was eating less, and even though I could see the scales dropping each week, I still looked in the mirror and saw fat. I couldn't explain it – but then anorexia is hard to understand.

I wasn't able to eat anything without checking the calorie content on the packet first. Flipping the food packet over to check the calorie content was a tic in itself. I started to believe food companies were lying to me, or may have made a mistake about the calories stated on the pack, so would round up the calories to the nearest whole number to make sure they hadn't under-calculated the true amount. Afterwards, I'd fill a notebook with all the foods I'd eaten that day and total them up. If I went over by just one calorie, it would send me into a meltdown. I'd work out for hours in tears to burn any extra calories I may or may not have consumed, often until I felt like fainting, or until I needed to lie on the gym floor to recuperate.

At sixteen, I was too young to have my own credit card, so I borrowed a friend's to buy cherry-flavoured diet pills off the internet that would swell up in your stomach when taken with water, which stopped you feeling hungry. I don't need to tell you how stupid and dangerous that was – Jesus Christ, people have died doing that very same thing. I took the recommended dose, but they didn't work, because they're designed for chronically obese people, and I was already anorexically thin, and so I'd take more – yet they still didn't work properly.

For a few weeks, I attempted the 'apple a day' diet, which is pretty self-explanatory, but because I had no energy it consisted of me having to skip lessons and sleep all day. My skin broke out and my headaches were horrendous. Instead of studying, most of my time was spent googling the calorie intake of food, or browsing images of thin women for 'thinspiration'. Name a popular food choice and I could reel off the calorie amount in each packet like some sort of anorexic Rainman. Pro-ana websites – online forums where girls encourage each other to be thin – became a refuge, and only they seemed to understand how my brain operated.

I was completely hooked on numbers and weight loss. Deep down, I knew I was crazy, but these forums made me feel just that *tiniest* bit sane. Other people obsessed over numbers as much as I did. Girls (and boys) would discuss various outlandish diets, posting photos of how much weight they were losing, and I'd feel like a failure in comparison. In fact, if I so much as dared to type 'I want help for my eating disorder', people would make out I was 'weak' for not being able to keep up with them. How sick is that? I thought these anonymous users were part of a supportive network, but in reality the sites were just a competition of who could become the thinnest.

I now not only felt like a failure in real-life, but online, too.

Mark never did break up with me properly. He cheated on me with none other than Sarah Davies – you know, Joe's girlfriend and my first girl kiss who I didn't actually want to kiss. She rang me up crying, saying it was a mistake, and then Mark called and said how sorry he was.

So I, being the desperately insecure girl I was, forgave him, of course. It wasn't Mark's fault at all! It was Sarah's. She was a nutter anyway, wasn't she?

Then, one day, Dave the Woman and I discovered Mark was throwing a party – a party that his alleged girlfriend, aka me, was not invited to. Joe messaged me asking what time we were getting to the party.

Mark's having a party? I typed.

Yes . . . Joe said, then must've realized I hadn't been invited.

Awkward.

Dave and I rocked up to her house that weekend and watched through the upstairs window as hordes of girls pulled up to the party that Mark was hosting in the field behind – which was owned by Dave's mum, the cheeky git! He was already stoned and drunk by this point and totally revelling in the attention.

'Who the hell does he think he is?!' I snapped.

We drank some vodka for a bit of Dutch courage, then made our way down. There were about fifty people there by this point, setting up tents on Dave's mum's land.

His face dropped when he saw us.

'W-what the hell are you doing here?!' he slurred.

'I could ask you the same question,' Dave said. 'This isn't even your field. It's my mum's.'

Jennifer – the girl whose beauty Mark had frequently told me about – suddenly appeared out of nowhere, wrapping her arms round *my* boyfriend's shoulders. She was undeniably stunning, with huge rosy lips and thick blonde hair. I'd heard she had done some modelling in the past, and that she had had sex with loads of boys, so all the boys fancied her. I hated her even more.

Mark then put his arm round Jennifer's waist while she giggled into her hand. *Hee-hee-hee*, I thought angrily. *You won't be laughing when I punch you in the effin' mouth.*

'I'm meant to be your girlfriend,' I said in a tone that was equally sad, hurt and confused.

'You're not any more,' he said. 'I thought you'd back off when you heard about me and Sarah, but no. Why are you obsessed with me? You're just . . . you're just . . . *frigid*.' He began chuckling at his own 'joke' and Jennifer joined in, looking up at him, doe-eyed. Joe, who'd told me about the party, was watching nervously from the side.

'F*ck off,' I said to Mark.

'Oh, whatever, Charli,' Mark replied. 'Why don't you go and make yourself sick again?'

The party seemed to fall silent all of a sudden, though in retrospect I think the blood in my body had boiled so much that it drowned the sound out.

How did Mark know about my secret?!

A fist came out of nowhere and hit Mark right in the jaw. Mine, in case you were wondering. Jennifer gasped. Mark looked gobsmacked. It left a huge red mark on his cheek.

No one knew what to say.

'Come on,' Dave said, and led me away to her house. Later, Dave's mum stormed down there and called Mark a dickhead, telling everyone to take their tents down and get off her land.

Restricting what I eat has always been a coping mechanism for me. Whenever times got tough or too much, I'd starve myself. And when things were *really* bad, I was starving myself and making myself sick as well. As you do.

I may have thought I was in control of my body, but I couldn't have been further from control if I'd tried. My mind was crumbling from the teenage pressures around me, and my only way of dealing with it was by not eating, or throwing what I had eaten up.

I know what heartbreak feels like. Trust me, I do. An ex's face plays round and round in your head like a broken record, popping up at inconvenient moments and making it difficult to concentrate on things. You feel physically sick from the top of your heart down to the pit of your stomach, wondering how you'll ever get over them or this feeling. You look at their social media pages, waiting to see which girl's photos they'll start 'liking' next. You think you'll never get someone better, or love anyone like that again.

But, somehow, even though you think you'll never recover, you *will* get over them. You will get somebody else. I can say this with the utmost certainty, because Mark is one of a few boys in my life I thought I'd never, ever, *ever* get over – and now he's just a ghost of my teenage past.

Also, you know the saying 'The heart wants what the heart wants'? Well, that's not entirely true. A lot of that has to do with your brain, actually.

Here's my (non-scientific) theory. If it truly came down to what your heart wanted, it would want to feel loved. Am I right? (Yes. Yes, I am.) It would want someone who cared about it – not someone who enjoyed smashing it to smithereens or who messed it about. It's your brain that likes to play tricks on you and make you believe that this person is right for you, when your heart and gut instinct say otherwise. So who are you going to listen to? Did I listen to my heart, or the Brain Deviant?

Take a wild guess!

On top of my obsession with food, I was now obsessed with Mark and his whereabouts. Thanks to the invention of social media, I stalked him constantly, and that exacerbated my anxiety and low self-esteem even further.

He loved posting photos of his latest squeeze, which, at one point, was a new girl practically every week. It would break my heart seeing photos of new girls on his social media accounts, but I was hooked on looking it up, as though it would somehow make me feel better. (It never did.)

Other boys began taking an interest in me – boys who were far more kind and funny and genuine than Mark ever was – but I wasn't interested. I just wanted him. In fact, the more he didn't want me, the more I fawned over him.

He wouldn't answer my calls. He would no longer speak to me online at night. He literally completely disappeared from everyday life, yet remained incredibly active online. It didn't make any sense. I'd been watching what I ate and had been losing weight. I wasn't as fat as I once had been. What was there not to fancy?

Now, with the added of bonus of Mark dumping me, the eternal arguments with my parents, hating boarding school and my dad gone for yet another billion months, my eating disorders and body image became worse. It became a game of *How Much Can I F*ck Myself Up?* except there were no winners, only a loser, and that loser was me.

I needed to reinvent myself and have a complete image overhaul. I wanted to become the girl I thought boys would fawn over – the Angelina Jolie types, who smoked and who had men hanging on to every word they said. OK, I wasn't at my desired weight yet, but I could change other things.

First off, I began getting piercings – weird and wonderful piercings in the most painful places possible, like the back of the neck and, on one particularly rough weekend, my wrist (I mean, WTF?). I liked the relief I felt once the needle went through my skin. I got my tongue pierced one Saturday as a way of not being able to eat for a week. It worked, but my tongue was throbbing and swollen for days. I dyed my hair black and wore kohl around my eyes, thinking I was some sort of femme fatale, when really I looked like a femme fail.

Then my behaviour in school got worse. One time, I went to the boys' school with this random girl I knew and smoked in the toilets. Can you imagine how much trouble I'd have been in if I got caught? Well, luckily I wasn't, but even if I had been caught I wouldn't have cared. I didn't care about anything.

I was in Heartbreak Mode, where all I could think about was *Mark, Mark, Mark*. Although I came across fine from the outside, deep down I was truly beside myself.

I cried about him before I closed my eyes and dreamt about him in my sleep. This was the man I was destined to be with; I was sure of it. It was just he didn't know it yet. I had visions of him driving to my house with a dozen red roses (though I'm not sure where that came from, seeing as he had yet to learn to drive) and begging me for forgiveness, telling me what a prat he'd been, and how I was the only girl for him. And then, out of the generosity of my heart, I'd graciously welcome him back.

I'd like to tell you Mark was the only boy in my life I've obsessed over, but of course he wasn't. When you're as insecure as I was, you're drawn to these characters like an addict, because their words and treatment of you confirm any doubts you ever had about yourself to begin with. Hurting yourself won't ever help you, but you don't care. You become hell-bent on destroying yourself, because what's the point? If they don't want you, who else will?

When you're that insecure, and once you've learnt to hate yourself that much, it's very difficult to snap out of that mindset. How do you magically erase the effects of bullying like I'd dealt with in Belgium, or the feeling that you've never been able to form relationships properly because you move all the time, or the chronic homesickness, or the fact you're a hideous and ugly person inside and out, or that the so-called love of your life doesn't want you?

Well, you can't. Not straight away anyway. You need to address your problems bit by bit, one by one. The last thing you need when you're at a low point is someone coming into your life and making your nerves worse, or believing a relationship will cure any insecurities you have about yourself. I can assure you that they won't.

You know those parties you read about in the newspapers, where teenagers post an invite on the internet and then a million people decide to show up and trash it out of the blue? Well, let me tell you about a now-infamous party called Dave's Rave, which actually made the local papers, and became somewhat of a local legend. (A legend to us, maybe, but not to Dave's mum.)

It all started when Dave the Woman got a phone call from her mum, telling her she was going on a very posh detox holiday to Jamaica during the Christmas holidays (or, in other words, doing a juice fast for two weeks with a bit of yoga), and because Dave was now a responsible seventeen-year-old, she was allowed to stay at home all by herself with a couple of friends. This was the best news we'd ever heard – it meant staying in a nice house on our own with some money for food (i.e. vodka) and other necessities (wine).

'We should have a get-together!' I announced one evening as Dave and I chatted in my dorm room (now-infamous last words). It was a genius idea. Having a get-together would mean Dave and I would be viewed as sophisticated socialites. It also gave me the opportunity to try to win back Mark, who I was still convinced was the love of my life, despite the fact he was mugging me off left, right and centre.

Dave and I spent the next few weeks planning and curating a list of the people (mainly fit boys) we were going to invite. It was the most exciting thing to happen to a couple of schoolgirls bored of being confined within the walls of a boarding school in Wales. We told our parents that we were going to Dave's to study. How they ever bought this with my behavioural record, I don't know – but it worked. Our plan was underway!

I hadn't seen Mark for around three months by this point, but I still thought about him daily, building him up in my head like some demigod. And religiously stalked his MySpace page, but whatever. I needed to show him how mature and glamorous I'd become.

*

It was the Christmas holidays, two days after Christmas to be exact, and I had just arrived at Dave's house with a couple of friends, ready for the party of the century. I loved Dave's manor house, though it felt weirdly bigger without her mum there. We couldn't have felt more grown-up being alone there if we tried. Dave and I squealed with excitement in the kitchen. Weeks of party planning were finally coming to life!

We'd posted an announcement on MySpace, and the party was going to take place the next day.

But some random friend of Mark's called Craig, who was 'MySpace famous' (he had about 20,000 'friends' on there), also wrote about the party, posting the address and telling people to BYOB. Dave and I had never met Craig personally, but we did know that if he came to your party it would be considered cool. Rather than see this as a potential problem, we viewed it as though a Kardashian was about to rock up.

As part of our epic weekender, Mark, George and a few other friends were going to stay with us the night before the party. God, we felt grown-up, having a sleepover with actual BOYS!

The doorbell rang, and I answered the door to Mark and George. I'd preened myself beforehand so that I looked perfect. I felt butterflies as Mark strolled through the front door, looking like some sort of model, but I tried to play it cool. I wanted to show him what a strong, sexy and independent woman he was missing out on and, most importantly, one who no longer vomited all over the floor in his presence.

'How much money has your mum left you, Dave?' George asked.

'A hundred pounds,' Dave replied.

'That's more than enough for alcohol then,' Mark said.

'Well, some of that has to go on food . . .' Dave began, but Mark and George began reeling off the alcohol brands they could buy with all that money, which we had never actually tasted but pretended to know about.

'How many people have you invited?' I asked them both, and I could've sworn Mark gave George a 'look', but I wasn't too sure.

'Just a couple,' Mark said. As though by magic, two of Mark's friends rocked up. We downed some drinks for a few hours, laughing and having a whale of a time.

'Here's to a great party!' George announced, and we cheered.

As we all camped out in Dave's mum's bedroom that night, I turned to Dave in the dark.

'I don't think this is such a good idea,' I whispered.

'It's too late to cancel it now!' Dave replied. 'Anyway, what could possibly go wrong?!'

The next day, we went to buy alcohol for the party. Picture me, Dave and a group of emo lads outside Sainsbury's handing me wads of notes. I was all dolled up in one of Dave's mum's expensive designer dresses. Dave had helped me do my make-up, and for added effect sprayed some gross Chanel perfume on my neck to help me smell 'older', too.

None of us could drive, obviously, so the group of us had had to get the bus down there.

'Why do I have to do this?' I asked George, as Mark smoked a cigarette with the other lads against a wall.

'Because you're the one who looks the oldest,' George said. 'Girls always get served anyway. Go to a cashier who's a boy if you're worried.'

I bloody well didn't look older. I looked like a seventeen-year-old in an expensive designer dress and heels I couldn't walk in. I counted the notes: £160 in total, £100 of which was Dave's money. It wouldn't fit in my purse so I shoved it in my handbag like some sort of pimp.

'You'd better be waiting for me if I get chased out by security,' I hissed at George, as the others looked on. Mark didn't seem to care. I knew he thought I wasn't capable of getting the drinks. Part of me wouldn't have been surprised if he wanted me to get caught by security.

'We're not going anywhere!' George said reassuringly as some old woman walked past. 'I'll come in with you and help choose the drinks anyway to begin with.'

I took in a huge breath and George and I marched into Sainsbury's with a trolley. We wandered down the alcohol aisle, my heart pounding. If you've ever been underage and tried to place bottles of wine, vodka and beer into a trolley as inconspicuously as possible, you'll know how scary it is.

'See you outside,' George said, then pulled his hoodie over his cap and walked out.

This was it. I was on my own now. I pulled my dress down and pushed my boobs up. Taking a deep breath, I walked to the till, pushing the trolley full of alcohol. *Find a male cashier*, I thought to myself, scanning the checkouts.

I found my prey! A checkout guy who couldn't have been older than twenty-one, with a floppy brown fringe and acne problem. Here went nothing.

The checkout guy looked at my boobs first, then my face.

'Hello,' he said. My heart was racing. Any minute now, he'd call security – I just knew it.

'Hello there!' I answered in the poshest voice known to (wo)man, placing the bottles of alcohol on to the conveyer belt. 'How are you, dear?'

'Could be better, like,' he said, and began scanning the bottles. 'Do you need help with your b–'

'No, no!' I replied quickly. 'I can quite manage myself.' Pause. 'Kind sir.'

Kind sir?! The 1800s called – they want their phrase back.

'I'm actually having a party tonight,' I said, hoping to distract him with conversation. 'I've just bought a house in the local area and was having a bit of a gathering.'

Beep. Beep. No reply from Mr Checkout Guy. Was I being convincing enough?

'You're more than welcome to join!' I said anxiously.

There was a pause.

'That'll be £143.50, please,' he said. Mr Checkout Guy looked at me in a way that said, '*Pay up now and get out.*'

'W-what? Oh yes, right. Of course.' I handed him the bunches of crumpled ten- and twenty-pound notes from my handbag and smiled. 'Well, that should be enough. Good day to you.'

I didn't even wait for the change. I grabbed the bags and legged it, rushing past a security guard with the sound of clinking beside my legs. OH MY GOD!!! I'd only gone and bloody done it!

'No *way*,' Mark said quietly as I walked out of the store.

'You legend!' George said as I held the bags up with a smile. *Screw you, Mark! I knew I could do it.* As if. I still secretly wanted him, even if he was being mean.

Once we got into the house, we made our way to the kitchen and began to crack open some vodka and Diet Coke. Much to my delight, Mark's latest girlfriend showed up not long after – I couldn't quite keep up with what number he was on now – and while some boys told me how 'great' I looked, he didn't say a thing. Oh, wait, he did say one thing actually when his girlfriend's back was turned:

'Your boobs look massive.'

What a guy.

At 8 p.m. the party was quietly underway. Any boys I'd ever remotely had a crush on had arrived, which was nice for me, and one boy had travelled up all the way from Brighton to be there. People were cracking open the drinks, Dave had poured snacks into a bowl and some guy called Death Jesus (a ginger guy with a beard who dressed like a goth) was completely stoned in the corner. In our naivety – and also in our defence – we truly believed that around thirty people would show up. Besides, everyone who'd arrived so far was very nice.

To fast-forward the events of the evening, I'd gone upstairs to chat to someone for half an hour when suddenly the party sounded very loud outside the bedroom door.

I poked my head out.

'*Oh my f***ing God.*'

It was manic. Standing in Dave's house were around two hundred lads who we'd never seen before, dressed in tracksuits and swigging cans of lager, yelling loudly. They were all aged about fifteen up – some of them looked like they were in their mid-twenties. Where the hell did they come from?!

I ran to Dave's bedroom, trying to find her, to discover that it had already been ransacked. There were muddy footprints all across the expensive cream carpet. Mine and Dave's iPods had been nicked, as well as Dave's hair straighteners, and her money box had been smashed everywhere. Some girl I'd never met before was staring at herself in the mirror.

'Some boys just tried to steal your Ugg boots but I told them to put them down,' she said, as though she was doing me some kind of favour. I hid my new boots in a cupboard and ran out again, trying to find Dave.

'Coming through!' I yelled, squeezing myself through the hordes of people on the stairs. Where the hell was she?!

God – so many people, swigging out of cans and yelling and chanting. I ran outside to the hot tub, which was now somehow a pitch-black colour with beer cans floating on top. How could this have happened in such a short space of time?!

'DAVE!' I yelled, running back into the house. '*DAAVVEEEE!!!*'

The house was totally trashed from top to bottom. Mirrors were either broken or covered in beer. Someone had ripped the sofa with a knife and smashed photos. I eventually found Dave in the kitchen, looking petrified. She was lodged between some guys in their thirties who were snorting cocaine on the kitchen table.

She rushed over to me and I led her out into the hallway. She glanced around at the hordes of people and began hyperventilating. I tried to console her, but kind of understandably she lashed out and slapped me across the face.

'Wahheeyyyy!' the lads yelled, but Dave was having a panic attack.

'GET! OUTTTT!!!' she yelled furiously, throwing her hands to her face.

Rather than make them leave, this thrilled them even more. They began cheering. We couldn't find our phones so she tried ringing the police on the landline, but the phone line had been cut. I rallied George and a couple of other people together, telling them to spread the word that the police were on their way.

'*THE POLICE ARE COMING!*' people began to yell, and this scared the idiots the most. It wouldn't have surprised me if half the boys here had already been in juvey anyway.

I ran outside to the front of the house. Some boys were sat in Dave's mum's Mercedes convertible, trying to get it to start – how they opened the door, I have no idea, as we later found the car keys in the kitchen drawer.

'GET THE F*CK OUT!' I yelled, and weirdly they did clamber out. There were dozens of suitcases scattered across Dave's front yard, full of expensive stolen goods, like silver photo frames and lamps and jewellery, but people were legging it down the country road before the mythical 'police' could get there. Once all the thugs had left, the rest of us were left standing in shock amongst the wreckage.

I don't think we realized how trashed the house was. All the doors in Dave's house were made out of solid wood, and someone had smashed a couple in half – I have no idea how, but it would've taken some effort. Dave's sister's room was totally destroyed – the cupboard doors had been ripped off, clothes stolen and her piggy bank smashed – and someone had broken into the attic. We got one of the boys to check and see if anyone was still up there. In one room, someone had thrown a crate of beer into the wall, leaving a huge dent in it. There was liquid all over the walls and mattress. Jelly beans had been thrown everywhere for a finishing touch.

'We are so dead,' Dave said, crying. 'I need to ring my dad.'

Dave's dad lived a few miles away in a nearby town, but it was around midnight now.

'Don't!' I said, snatching the phone off her. 'We need to try and fix some of this ourselves. Everyone can help clean up, can't we, guys? It's not . . . too bad, I suppose?'

Everyone nodded and agreed, though how we'd ever clean this mess up, I didn't know. There was a solid cream carpet that ran throughout the entire house and it was completely trashed with burn marks, wine stains and other fluids probably not worth mentioning.

'Look, maybe we can pay for some expensive cleaners to come and fix it?' I said hopefully. 'How much does a cleaner cost? We can lie and say Mark got drunk and fell into the door and broke it . . .'

Speaking of Mark – where was he? Oh yeah, that's right: he'd legged it an hour or so ago, hiding back at his house. Everyone was scrambling around to help mend and clean whatever broken thing they could find, but he'd run off in the heat of the moment. We tried calling him to help but he rejected all our calls. In that moment, any attraction I felt for him disappeared. It appears I can fancy boys who treat me like sh*t, but not wusses.

Everyone clambered in together to help clean that night. I will never forget the sight of my campest gay friend dancing and hoovering to the sound of Jay-Z's 'Big Pimpin'', which couldn't have misdescribed that evening further if we'd tried. We were going to be in so much trouble. Despite our best cleaning efforts, the house was royally f***ed. The following morning, we called Dave's dad to come round, who, despite having been divorced from Dave's mum for a while now, went mental on her behalf. Within a few minutes, he'd called Dave's aunt, who came round to inspect the damage.

'WHAT THE HELL HAVE YOU DONE?!' she yelled. 'YOU LOT – GET THE HELL OUT OF MY SISTER'S HOUSE!!!'

We legged it as quickly as we could. I and a few others had to get a bus back to the train station in the pouring rain. Because it was the Christmas holidays, none of the trains were running; eventually, I got home around five hours later, to my screaming dad who currently had my family round for a post-Christmas tea.

In case you were wondering, we caused over £30,000 worth of damage.

'You could've thrown Dave's Rave when I was there,' Dave's sister said disappointedly when we got back to school.

8

THE YEAR WE DO NOT TALK ABOUT

I was a misfit.

I was now at an age where being naughty was no longer acceptable or considered 'a bit of fun'. As you know, I'd always been mischievous, but this time I'd well and truly gone too far. I could no longer hide behind the innocence of childhood and had to take responsibility for my actions. I'd helped cause £30,000 worth of damage in somebody else's home, after all.

After Dave's Rave, it seemed like everyone had had enough of me. It could've been paranoia, but I couldn't shake the feeling that friends were distancing themselves from me. Adults kept reiterating the fact I was on a 'slippery slope', or making out that I was one teenage pregnancy away from an ASBO, which didn't exactly inspire me to be better behaved. If enough people tell you what a pain in the arse you are, or how you're not going to amount to very much if you continue this way, you'll finally end up believing them.

I believed I was worthless, and so I treated myself badly. The eating disorders, the bad behaviour, the low self-esteem were all connected, but all I could see were separate issues with one thing in common: me.

The other problem about being known for your behavioural issues or for getting into trouble is that some people like to hide behind you when the going gets tough. It's easier to blame you for everything that goes wrong, than to woman up and take some of the rap. I was used to being in trouble. Not a week went by when I wasn't told off for something, large or small. When other girls got into trouble it was as though the world had come to an end. Their parents would scream at them down the phone saying how disappointed they were in them, whereas mine were just used to it by this stage.

However, unlike a lot of parents, my mum and dad were very honest about the fact I wasn't an angel. Whenever I'd get into trouble with someone, they'd often sit back and listen while parents complained about how I'd led their precious little darlings astray. I used to wish that my parents would argue back and defend me more, but they never really did. But now that I'm older I'm grateful that they didn't always defend me. They didn't blow hot air up my backside and lead me to believe I could blame other people for a situation that went wrong, when I was equally to blame. I was being taught the importance of owning my mistakes.

Not long after Dave's Rave, for example, I got invited to the most boring house party *ever*. I'd been invited by a girl called Faye, who was one of those girls who loved letting me take the blame for things that went wrong, and her parents did, too. They were so bad that my dad actually told her parents to stop blaming me for everything that went wrong, and they stormed off in a huff. (Thanks, Dad!)

I wanted to leave twenty minutes after arriving there. The Playboy Mansion this was not. I was sat in a room with boys who I doubted could *spell* the word vagina, let alone had seen one. Midway through the evening, some guy got a packet of white powder out and asked if I wanted a line. I said no, then left. Later I was told that it wasn't cocaine – he was an idiot who'd been mugged off by a dealer who'd clearly sold him crushed-up paracetamol. What a prat!

The day after the party, Faye deleted me from her social media accounts, telling me her parents didn't want me hanging around with her any more. Someone had stolen jewellery from the party and her mum was filing a police report; Faye had the cheek to ask me if I'd done it (I'm a lot of things, but not a thief). Her parents also found out there'd been 'cocaine' at the party, and because Faye saw me talking to the guy who had it, they naturally assumed I'd had something to do with it. I started to wish that people would realize that underneath the facade I was a good girl, after all.

Since my praying phase had ended, I hadn't thought about God at all really. Lauren the Goth read satanic poems in her dorm room at night, but religion didn't play on my mind that much. I didn't come from an overly religious family, but each morning in assembly we'd have to sing religious hymns and pray. Because of my behavioural problems and the pressure this was putting on my mum, I was constantly made to feel I was doing wrong. I then began to wonder if God was watching my every move, creating bad karma for me every time I messed up, or if he thought I was a sinner. If I smoked down by the garages, which had become a daily occurrence by this point, I began to wonder if I'd go to hell for it. Good girls didn't smoke, did they?

I hadn't applied for confirmation with the girls in my year. But when the girls in the year below were asked if they wanted to go ahead and do it, I jumped at the chance. For the longest time, I'd been made to feel like a nightmare. This was a chance for me to be holy – the type of daughter to be proud of. Now was my chance to be good.

I wanted to make my parents proud. I was so tired of being a difficult part of their lives. Anorexia is typically a selfish illness, but I didn't *want* to upset them – it just happened.

I was anxious on the day of my confirmation. I wore a beautiful pink fifties-style dress and pink cardigan, looking like butter wouldn't melt. I was so nervous that when I got to the altar I forgot to bow to the vicar, and quickly spun round to correct myself, bowing awkwardly. I truly hoped no one had noticed, but my headmaster had all right.

I may have thought a man in the sky was looking down on me, but luckily there was someone in human form doing it for him.

'I knew you'd mess up,' the headmaster whispered as I went to sit back down.

I guess the underlying factor in all of my eating disorders was that I wasn't happy, and hadn't been for as long as I could remember. So much of that was down to how I felt about myself. I mean, let's face it – if I was a happy person, I wouldn't have been purposefully starving myself, would I? Happy people don't do things like that. They do things like surround themselves with friends, or other happy things, like yoga. And I did neither.

My anxiety repeatedly told me how unliked I was and that no one wanted to hang around with me, so I didn't see the point of making any effort. And because I hadn't eaten properly for such a long time, not only was I no fun to hang out with, but I barely had the energy to walk across the school campus, let alone balance on my bloody head.

The irony was that I *still* truly believed that becoming thinner would make me happier and solve all my self-esteem problems – and did it heck! Eating disorders made me even *more* nervous, and even *more* upset, and even *more* isolated. Obsessively watching what I ate created problems, rather than solved any. But the cycle just continued, and that goal weight was always reducing, and always out of reach. When nobody was looking, I'd cry in my dorm, wanting to pull my hair out from the anxiety.

People didn't know how to act around me. They eventually gave up knocking on my bedroom door and inviting me to breakfast or to any other mealtimes because my answer would always be: 'I'm not hungry.' Then, in some other bizarre twist, the Brain Deviant would tell me the reason no one knocked on my door any more was because no one wanted to hang out with me, so I'd stay in my room and not socialize with anyone at all. I even stopped hanging around with Dave the Woman, convinced she hated me, too. I once overheard some friends talking about me in the common room and about how they'd tried to get me help, but how I'd refused it. Like I said earlier: you can't help people who don't want to help themselves.

I'm not a doctor, but in my experience eating disorders do not stem from nowhere. You don't just wake up one day and think, *I know! Today I'm going to make myself sick for no reason!* or, *I wonder how many hours I can go without eating, just for the lolz!* They develop from a combination of factors, but predominantly low self-worth: the feeling of never being good enough or 'right'; the type of personality to please and to overachieve; creating an internal database of every negative or mean comment in your head so that you can never escape even the tiniest criticism; getting conflicting messages from the things you see and read in your day-to-day; and other pressures.

Everyone handles things in different ways, but when I had anorexia and bulimia I'd become overwhelmed by these things. The thoughts built up in my head and consumed me, like I was drowning in a pool and couldn't come up for air. The list of reasons why a person has an eating disorder can be endless, but it's important to remember that everyone who's dealt with one has their own issues to contend with, and to not judge them on that. Who's to say that one problem won't affect somebody else differently? You can't. Humans are complex, and everyone deals with problems individually.

However, I think it's important for me to reiterate how lucky and privileged I'd been in the grand scheme of things. In hindsight, my problems were no worse than those of the majority of teenagers across the country. In fact, I can say that they actually didn't match up at all. Sure, I didn't love school – but who did? And fine, I was growing up during a time that fetishized size zero – but so was everyone else! But there is no denying that my anxiety and eating disorders made the usual teenage stresses ten times worse. There are people in the world whose problems far surpassed my own, but who didn't end up starving themselves or abusing themselves as a coping mechanism. The fact I was able to restrict food and starve myself was, in a sick way, a *privilege*. I mean, in a world where I had access to food I also had the option of turning it away.

But I did have some issues that were big to me. For one, I felt well and truly abandoned. I didn't want to be in education and couldn't understand why I still had to attend this boarding school when my mum lived so close. In hindsight, I wasn't being abandoned at all: my parents wanted the best for me, and this school was one of the top in the entire country. But when you're sixteen or seventeen you don't care about how good your school allegedly is, or where it ranks in *The Times* Best School List. You want to feel *free*.

I'd have blazing rows that lasted for months and months with my mum and dad, where I begged to leave and go to a normal college near their house, but they refused. My housemistress would call me into her office repeatedly, telling me to carry on with school and not to give up now. After one particular argument my parents drove me back to school on a Sunday as a punishment. I hitch-hiked home in the car of some randomer I'd met down at the garage on the outskirts of my school's campus (another one of my bright ideas), and my mum and dad drove me straight back. My mum thought she had a problem child and so would get the school to deal with me; my dad was always away working, and she felt alone in having to handle my behaviour.

The deputy headmistress yelled at me in her office and told me I was acting selfishly, which, when you hate yourself enough already, isn't really what you want to hear.

Isn't it funny how things are viewed differently at the time and then in hindsight? In my teens, I genuinely believed nobody liked me. I genuinely believed people didn't have my back. But so much of that insecurity was down to me and my issues. I'd later hear down the grapevine that people thought I was funny and caring in school – none of the traits I believed I possessed.

They might've thought I was a dickhead at times, because I undoubtedly could be, but the girls in my class did actually have my back – more than my teenaged insecure self cared to admit. For example, there was the time I got caught smoking in the art block, and a girl managed to persuade the teacher I needed the cigarette for an 'art project', or the time I smoked in my dorm room and the smell reeked the entire corridor out, and my friends helped spray deodorant everywhere so that I didn't get in trouble or set the fire alarm off. There was also the time I ordered a fake ID from the internet and it accidentally got sent, nameless, to the headmaster's assistant, but my friend was in the office at the time and managed to grab it before he studied the card properly.

But, like I often focused on the negatives ('*You're so ugly!*', '*You're useless!*', '*Your parents hate you!*'), I tended to dwell on and obsess over the opinion of girls who weren't so nice to me. That's the thing – you'll always meet some mean girls in life, and when we left school some girls truly began showing their colours. But there are also a load of great ones who aren't out to get you, and if you open your eyes wide enough, you'll notice them from a mile off.

I was heading back to my room one evening from the gym, exhausted from exercising on an empty stomach and feeling as angsty as I usually did when I needed to make myself sick and didn't want to be caught, when I saw that there was a note stuck on my door.

Fancy a chat? My office. 7 p.m. X

I recognized the handwriting straight away and my stomach dropped. It was from my housemistress, who was the scariest teacher in the entire school. Since she had become my sixth-form housemistress I'd tried to stay out of her way as much as possible. To see an 'X' at the end of the note was the weirdest thing of all. Was she on crack?!

My anxiety yelled, *'YOU'RE IN TROUBLE!'* Like everyone with anxiety, I began overthinking everything I could've possibly done wrong, jumping to the worst conclusion imaginable. My mind went into overdrive. Had I said something bad without realizing?!

But my biggest fear, as silly as it sounds, was having my bulimia discovered. In a place where it often felt there was no privacy, it was the only thing I had that felt secret – the one thing I kept to myself. I was conflicted between wanting to be saved from this daily torment and wanting to be left alone to deal with it. Thanks, bulimia, for turning me into a madwoman.

I reluctantly went to her office for 7 p.m., mainly because I didn't want her to yell at me for not doing as I was told, and sat awkwardly on a spare chair. Her face looked soft and kind, but it didn't make me feel any less nervous. *Please don't mention my eating*, I thought.

'I got you some biscuits,' she said, offering me a plate of chocolate digestives and pink wafers. God, I wanted them. Biscuits had never looked so appealing. But my brain started to calculate the calories in each one, how hard I'd worked in the gym to burn the calories, and how long it would take me to burn them off. In the end, I figured it wasn't worth it.

'Take one,' she said.

'I'm OK, honestly,' I replied, feeling a bit sweaty.

'*GO ON – EAT THE BISCUITS, YOU FAILURE!!!*' the Brain Deviant yelled, but I looked down at my lap.

'Your friends are worried about you,' she said sweetly. 'A few girls have come to me and told me you haven't been to any mealtimes and keep going to the gym excessively.'

Huh? What friends?! One girl knew about my eating disorder – if it hadn't been obvious from my no-show at every mealtime this term, it was when I'd accidentally forgotten to turn my laptop off and left the pro-ana forum on the screen. A friend came into my room and saw it, and had confronted me in private. I lied and said I'd looked at it for research, but the notebook I kept with all the images of anorexically thin women and my calorie counting said otherwise.

I could've sought help then, but I didn't. She offered me a lifeline but I refused to take it. When it comes to recovery you need to want to get better yourself, and I just wasn't ready. I was too obsessed with fitting into a UK size-six pair of jeans and sticking below 1,000 calories a day to let go of it.

But now, as I sat in my housemistress's office, I felt vulnerable. She was being so nice and sympathetic. I was so incredibly embarrassed that my secret was no longer just with me and my friend, but it was now known by my scary housemistress as well. My lungs wanted to explode and scream for help. This was the perfect opportunity to let the bulimia go. But the words just wouldn't come out.

'Do you make yourself sick?' she asked, and I felt even more put on the spot.

'No!' I said a little too quickly to be convincing. 'God, no. Why would I do that?'

'Well, you have lost a lot of weight,' she said.

She sounded concerned, but this made me feel ecstatic.

'Really?!' I said, trying not to sound thrilled.

'I think you should start going to the nurses' office at lunch and dinner,' she said. 'Just for the time being, and until you start eating normally again.'

Well, how could I argue with that?

The nurses would bring me lunch on a tray from the dining room. I'd have to sit there in their office among girls with colds and eat every bite, then show them it had disappeared. Like a toddler.

But one day, a few weeks in, a couple of bitchy girls in the year above saw me eating a plate of food on my own. I knew they'd start a rumour about me. And that's precisely what they did.

'You know she's rexy, right?' one of them said, deliberately loudly so I could overhear, in assembly a few days later. I stared at her with a face like thunder, and her expression went from bitchy to 'uh-oh'. First things first, 'rexy' isn't a nice term to describe someone. Secondly, making the whole world aware that someone has an eating disorder isn't cool, either.

I was mortified. That lunchtime I told the sisters I was well enough to start eating on my own again.

'I don't think you're ready yet . . .' one sister said.

'I definitely am,' I replied. 'I feel much better now, thank you.'

And, rather than get better, I slipped back into my old ways. I spotted a birthday cake in the house kitchen one day and began grabbing chunks of it with my bare hands, gobbling it down like there was no tomorrow while nobody else was looking, then threw it all up afterwards. When our housemistress threw a DVD night to celebrate the end of exams, with sweets and crisps and pizza and so many other wondrous things, I slipped out halfway through and threw up plates of that, too.

Because going to university was what you did, I reluctantly applied to Leeds University to study German and politics. I got in, much to my family's delight, but not mine. I'd been on a campus for the last six years of my life and I'd hated it. On top of that, studying a course that didn't interest me for a further three years was my idea of hell.

I was due to go to Leeds in a week. Everything had been bought – pots and pans, a new duvet, new clothes. But the idea of yet again being pressured into something I didn't want to do made me feel sick. I'd never experienced this level of anxiety. My skin was bubbling with angst and stress. I wanted to rip my hair out or pull my nails out with pliers. My gut was telling me going to Leeds was wrong, wrong, wrong, yet everyone in my family was thrilled that I was the first person in my family to go to university. If I quit, I'd be letting my entire family down – *again*.

But a few days before we were due to drive up there, my driving instructor had to stop the car. I literally couldn't breathe at the steering wheel.

'I'm not letting you kill us,' he said. 'What's going on? Your nerves are through the roof.' He made me get out of the car – my legs were shaking like jelly – and drove me home, telling my parents I needed to rest.

Soon, my anxiety turned into rage. I was sick of being told what to do. For once, I wanted to feel in control of my life and my destiny. Besides, I was eighteen now. I was an adult. I therefore knew everything. Right? I wanted to be a model, I'd been working on getting to my goal weight for years – what good would a degree be to me? I needed to be thinner, not better educated.

'I'm not going,' I said a couple of days before. 'I'm moving back to London to achieve my dreams.'

And so that's what I did. I ran away from all the problems in my head, when in reality they were still lingering there, following me like a bad omen.

Let's cut to the chase and say that the year following my departure from school is one of those parts in my history I'm choosing to brush over, just like I have a few other points in my story. I'll talk about them one day, but it was a very, very difficult time.

I can also tell you that because I didn't get professional help for my childhood anxiety, depression and eating problems, dealing with very adult situations threw me over the edge. I may have been eighteen, and I may have felt like I was capable of being an adult, but I wasn't. I was just as fearful and not in control of my life as I had been as a child.

The last thing you need when you're a jittery, insecure mess is to surround yourself with people who don't really want the best for you. Unfortunately, that's what I did. My so-called 'friends' only liked me when I was crazy and silly on a wild night out, but they didn't really have my back. True friends stick by you no matter what; these friends would stick by you if it gave them a fun story to tell.

But I wanted to be a model. I'd never wanted anything so desperately before. I'd gone to London with dreams of getting down to my goal weight and being signed, whisked away from my boring life, proving to my parents that I didn't need university. But life doesn't work like that, and the reality was worse than I could have imagined.

When was I going to learn that I was never going to find happiness in a pair of size-six jeans? That my obsession with starving myself was only making everything else in my life worse? I was addicted to abusing myself. I was addicted to people telling me what I already thought – that I wouldn't amount to anything, that I was a bad person who deserved horrible things to happen to her. Luckily, I managed to get out.

I knew I was dangerously close to the edge, so I staged a Grand Escape. The one thing I wanted more than anything was to be with my mum. And so that's where I went. My mum was living in the north of England by this stage, and when I got home I never wanted to leave. I'd hurt her, I'd done bad things, but I wasn't bad. I wanted to be good again.

*

This is the part of my story where every issue, problem, argument, mean comment or bad memory exploded in my brain like a puff of smoke, causing me to have a breakdown. What a bundle of laughs that was!

I couldn't get out of bed. I still couldn't eat. It was as though I was in a constant daze, where words echoed and nothing made sense. I can't remember where my dad was in all of this, but he doesn't feature in my memories of that time. Regardless, I can't remember a lot from the Year We Do Not Talk About, because it was as though my brain erased parts of it completely, eradicating the visual memories, but leaving the emotional pain behind.

Over time, I got flashbacks. This went on for weeks. I felt so safe being back home with my family, but numb when it came to thinking about the future and how I'd cope. I'd well and truly screwed up, with no one to blame but myself. I was a lost cause. Forget modelling. Forget being liked. I didn't care about a single damn thing. I'd be in the shower for an hour staring blankly at the tiles, or curled up in a ball crying endlessly until I had nothing left to give.

But even though I'd let her down, my mum was the one person who sorted me out. One day, she stormed into my room and told me I was getting a job.

'You've got to snap out of this,' she said. 'This isn't healthy.'

I was on anti-depressants by this point, so getting a job was the last thing I wanted to do. But she sat with me as we looked at the Job Centre website, making me apply for any job that would take me and my qualifications. One job popped up that was very well paid. To say it was niche was an understatement – it was selling water coolers. It wasn't sexy, but Mum convinced me that getting a job would make me feel better. And you know what – even though it was boring AF, my mum was right.

I'd distanced myself from the London crowd. I tried to pretend that none of the bad stuff had happened, that I was a good girl. And deep down, underneath all the craziness, I was – I'd just gone off the rails a bit. (Well, a lot.) These 'friends' would call me, wanting me to go out partying or raving or whatever, and I'd switch my phone off. I knew from their perspective me going AWOL was a very weird thing to do, even by my standards, but I had to push that period in time to the back of my mind.

But then I got an email from a particular 'friend' and photographer from those crazy months, Ed, telling me to call him ASAP. Ed was one of those friends you were never quite sure was really a mate at all, but if you caught him on a good day it was like you were the bestest friends ever.

Like me, he was up for doing crazy stuff. Unlike me, he was someone who liked to make people feel sh*t about themselves when they least needed it. (Then again, do they ever need to feel that way?) We'd lived together in a mansion in central London with this random rich man Ed had met online, never paying rent or following any rules. How we got away with that for months on end, I don't know. It was fun having no parental guidance at first, but eventually it became tiresome. It was a very hedonistic lifestyle, where we thought about nothing bar ourselves. We'd stay in the same clothes for days, go to weird parties and hang out with random celebrities, strippers and drag queens. Male models would randomly crash on the sofa, or a fight would break out between them. The millionaire had a different boyfriend every week, and would have screaming matches with most of them, throwing their stuff out on to the street.

Although Ed was one of the people I'd distanced myself from since my Grand Escape, this call seemed very urgent. I debated whether or not to call him back – he was probably drunk or high, as per usual, and would want me to join in one of his mad adventures. But I was desperately lonely by this stage. I hadn't seen or spoken to anyone my age in months. So I turned on the crazy Charli I knew he wanted to hear (or, more precisely, the only Charli he was interested in) and returned his call.

To cut a very long story short, the biggest modelling agency in the country at the time – actually, maybe the WORLD – wanted to meet me. *Me!* It all started when Ed showed my photos to a friend of his who worked there. (They weren't friends at all, just people who bumped into each other at parties then bitched about each other afterwards.) Apparently, she just had to meet me; I had such a 'strong' and 'unique' look. I doubt she would've thought the same thing had she seen me in my current state, sitting at the computer in tracksuit bottoms with bad skin and greasy hair tied into a bun.

'So when can you meet them?' he asked, and I heard him inhaling cigarette smoke.

I put on the charm all right. I put on the whole 'I couldn't give a sh*t' attitude and met Ed outside the Tube. I'd lied to my work and told them I was ill. Well, it wasn't like I'd care about skiving off from that dump once I was an international modelling superstar, was it?!

I hadn't seen Ed in months, and rather than seeming excited to see me he got straight to the point.

'Your hips . . .' he said disappointedly.

'Yeah? What's wrong with them?'

'They've got . . . quite big,' he said.

I hadn't noticed any weight gain when I looked in the mirror. I had tried to stay away from any triggers as much as I possibly could in an attempt to rid the harmful eating patterns from my brain on my own. I found it impossible not to weigh myself if I passed scales. I knew I only had to step on them once before becoming obsessed with them again.

Perhaps the weight gain was due to the anti-depressants I was on, but my bottom half was still only a size eight, at most. Nevertheless, Ed's comments didn't exactly gear me up for my big meeting. I may have been acting like I didn't care about being signed, but I massively cared. I was PETRIFIED. The Brain Deviant convinced me I was going to mess it up: my one lucky break. Now, though, I actually had Ed's comments to verify that fact.

Ed and I went into the agency and met the New Faces booker, who took us into a spare office to chat. My palms were dripping in sweat. Could she tell my voice was quivering? I hoped not. She asked me all the usual questions, like how old I was (Ed told me to lie and say I was seventeen, even though I was nineteen), what did I want to do in the future, did I have a job on the side . . . that kind of thing. She chewed gum the whole time and didn't seem to care that much. Well, why would she? I was just one of a sea of girls she'd meet daily who dreamt of making it big.

I was in there with her for ages, laughing in the right places and whatnot. Eventually she took some photos on a digital camera and went to show them to the rest of the team. After ten minutes of me and Ed messing about, she came back in the room.

'OK,' she said, still chewing gum loudly. 'Here's the deal. We think you're really strong, but your measurements are too big. I'm just being honest with you.'

'OK,' I replied, trying not to care, but inside I was mortified. Why the hell had I bothered coming if I was as big as they said I was?! My instincts were right all along. I was DISGUSTING.

'But I've spoken to the others, and we *looovvveee* your face.' I took what she said with a pinch of salt – she was about as genuine as a Louis Vuitton bag at a car-boot sale. 'However – if you get down to a thirty-four-inch hip, we'll take you on.'

Huh? What? Was she serious?

'Really?' I said, gobsmacked.

'Yeah,' she said, completely unbothered.

Oh my God! My heart was racing. I was ecstatic. For the first time in months, I was beaming.

'How big is a thirty-four-inch hip? I mean, what dress size is that?' I asked.

'About a UK size six,' she said, though I now know that it can sometimes be smaller. It all depends on the way you're built. 'So – do you think you can do it?'

I knew losing weight was going to be tough, but, hell yeah, was I up for the challenge! I guess I just hadn't pushed myself enough last time I was in school – and, besides, I'd got caught out starving myself anyway. This time would be different. This time I had an end goal: a life of success, popularity and happiness. There was reasoning behind my madness. It was my dream job and an excuse to get some control back in my life with dieting.

'I'll do it in a month,' I promised.

I couldn't concentrate on my job. I was too focused on losing weight, too blinded by the bright future that lay in front of me. We had notepads by the sides of our desks at work and I'd scribble my daily calorie intake in it, carefully making sure I never went over. I didn't care about selling water coolers anyway. Getting signed to this agency was the biggest thing I'd ever strived for, and I was not going to let anything get in the way. Screw university! Screw education! Most importantly, SCREW THIS JOB! Modelling was my future career, not this tripe.

I promised I wouldn't get ill this time – mentally, I mean.

'It's just a diet,' I reassured myself, though I wasn't too confident that I wouldn't slip back into my old bulimic ways. This was my one shot to make my dreams come true. A month would go by quickly. I had to give it all I had.

I found a calculator online that told me in order to get down to my goal weight I'd have to eat 800 calories a day. It did come with a health warning, saying this was dangerous, but who cared about health when I could become a model? I'd tried the zero-calorie-a-day diet, so I knew it couldn't be as bad as that, but I also know it wouldn't be as easy as a 1,200-calorie diet, either. I was eating something, right? That meant I couldn't be unhealthy. How hard could it be?

The first few days were fine. But soon my mood dipped so significantly that it threw me over the edge. I could barely concentrate on anything at work. Nothing was making sense on the screen, no matter how much I stared at it. Difficult?! This diet was torture. I was absolutely starving each and every day.

Before my mum dropped me off at work – she says before I'd even had breakfast – I'd start the day off by saying, 'What's for dinner tonight?' Saying those words was another obsession. You see, if I knew what we were eating that night, it would mean I could subtract that amount from my total allowance of 800 calories, then allow myself to eat the remaining calories during the day. God, I was a woman possessed.

Ed would text me frequently to see how my diet was getting on.

Amazing! I'd reply.

The reality was I was beyond moody, beyond starving and either yelled or cried all the time. Not exactly the lifestyle I'd envisioned.

I hadn't had time to think how I'd be able to sustain this diet when I got signed. I just thought I'd deal with it when the time came. However, a big fear of mine was knowing that if I started eating normally again – or even upped my intake by a few hundred calories – I'd balloon in weight. This is what happens. Your body tries to hold on to any fat it can save and your metabolism crashes, making it almost impossible to lose anything.

Not long after, guess what happened at work? I got fired. Yep. My boss had read my notebooks full of my obsessive calorie calculations and how much money I'd saved since working there, which I was going to use to live in London. He cried after he fired me, apparently. He said it was one of the hardest things he'd ever had to do because I was a 'very sweet girl'.

If only you knew, I thought.

God, another incident to let my family down. Fired at nineteen! What a failure. However, once I calmed down a bit, I saw this as a blessing in disguise. It meant I could focus on my modelling career that was, quite literally, inches from my grasp. Who needed water coolers anyway? (No one, it turned out. It was the recession.)

So, each day, I'd wake up at seven thirty, do some exercises in my room, then walk Belle the dog twenty minutes to my grandparents' house. That was the only exercise I could muster. It felt strenuous, and although I was simply walking I was always out of breath. The more weight I lost, the harder it got. I ignored the heart palpitations and blue and purple nails from malnutrition. By the time I got to my grandparents' I'd fall asleep on the sofa – I was sleeping all the time, because my body was essentially shutting down.

'Let me drive you back,' my grandad would offer.

'No!' I'd snap, like he'd suggested the worst thing on earth. 'I need to walk! I need the exercise!'

The other thing my grandparents had, and which my mum had banned from the house, were bathroom scales: one in the downstairs toilet, and one upstairs. The moment I'd arrive, I'd scramble to the downstairs bathroom, take off my baggy clothes (tight-fitting clothes were never gonna happen) and stand on them naked, stepping on and off repeatedly to check what my exact weight was. Everything had to be removed – how could I be sure a necklace didn't weigh an extra pound, let alone socks?! Then I'd go upstairs and do the same to make sure the number on both scales matched. I couldn't be too sure if one was lying to me or not. One, two, three, four, five – on, off, on, off until I had a number I was satisfied with.

Week by week, the scales were going down. Each time the ticker dropped closer to zero, adrenaline rushed through my body, like I was on a drug high. I'd never felt such euphoria. I was addicted to being thin, and no number was small enough. If the numbers went down, I'd be high on cloud nine. But if the weight stalled, or if the ticker went back up, I would positively lose my sh*t.

People, especially women, can gain weight for numerous reasons. It's not as simple as just eating less and expecting the scale to go down. The main reason for weight gain each month is hormones – I think you can gain up to five pounds before your period, sometimes more (yay! It's so great being a woman). Salt is another 'false' weight – eat something salty, and your body will retain water and make you feel squishy. Drinking water can also make you temporarily weigh more. It's a trick I used to fool the nurses when they weighed me, even though they soon caught on and made me go to the loo beforehand to make sure I hadn't cheated.

These 'bad days', as I called them in my diary, turned me into a madwoman (as though I wasn't one already). I'd go BALLISTIC. I'd be in a horrific mood all day and would deliberately eat less in the hope I wouldn't have such a bad day tomorrow.

'*FAILLLUUUURREEEE!*' the Brain Deviant would yell.

'Would you like a biscuit?' my nan would offer.

'NO!' I'd yell, then would storm upstairs and do a bunch of sit-ups or squats, thinking that would somehow make a world of difference. My skin would itch from how irritated and frustrated I was with myself. Within an hour, my mood would be calm again. Mood swings are just one of the problems you have when you starve yourself.

'*YOU'RE PATHETIC!*' the Brain Deviant would yell. '*YOU CAN'T DO ANYTHING RIGHT! NO WONDER NO ONE LOVES YOU! NO WONDER*

YOU HAVE NO FRIENDS! NO WONDER YOU'RE SO UGLY!'

A month to the day passed, and I wasn't down to my target weight. I had well and truly f***ed up. I wondered what Ed would've thought about me. I couldn't even get weight loss right.

I was about four pounds from what I liked to call 'perfect'. Except that's the thing with eating disorders – you can hit that goal weight, and it'll never be enough. You're chasing happiness. A number on a scale will never solve that.

When are you going back in? Ed would text me.

'Just give me another couple of weeks,' I promised.

But the weight just wouldn't budge. My body was essentially going WTF and trying to hold on to any weight it could to protect my organs. The fact I'd lost over a stone and a half in four weeks was not good enough for me, nor was the fact that old clothes hung off me. I was a big fat failure, and the Brain Deviant never let me forget it.

My eating disorder was ravaging my body. Looks-wise, you become far from pretty. You constantly look tired. Your breath smells. You break out in spots because of the lack of nutrients. Your skin looks grey. Your hair falls out.

And guess what? You're never, ever happy.

What I saw in the mirror wasn't 'fat', really. It was just a weight of issues: a heavy burden of guilt, shame and loneliness topped up with a nice dose of anxiety in human form. That was why I felt fat. But when I looked in the mirror, although I did see a distorted view of my body, I really just saw a let-down.

By week seven – almost a month after I'd promised I'd be 'ready' – I decided to bite the bullet and head back to the agency. I wasn't sociable. I wasn't happy. I was in bed by 6 p.m. every night. How much more ready could I be?

I was two pounds heavier than I wanted to be when I met Ed at the same spot outside the Tube, but I weighed less than I ever had before. It was now or never.

Rather than point out my faults, this time Ed seemed . . . impressed.

'Wow,' he said. 'You look great.'

I didn't look great. My head looked like a moon on a stick, my skin dull and lifeless, even with lashings of foundation. But Ed rarely gave compliments, so I knew he must've thought I was now 'model material'. He'd spent a lot of our alleged 'friendship' telling me how fat I was, or how small my boobs were, or if I changed X/Y/Z I'd be the 'perfect model'.

The Fake-AF Booker from before came to greet me. She eyed me up and down.

'Let's measure you then,' she said, taking out a measuring tape. Like Ed, she also seemed impressed. A wave of relief fell over me. The numbers did all the talking. My tummy was rumbling loudly – I hadn't eaten anything that morning in the hope the measurements would somehow drop further.

'Let me get some of the team to come in,' she said.

Once again, I sat in the empty office, staring at the endless magazine covers featuring my favourite supermodels. One by one, the agents came in and chatted to me – about four or five in total. Some would bitch about the famous supermodels, though I was pretty convinced they wouldn't say those kind of things to their faces. I nodded and laughed, hoping I was saying the right things.

I glanced at the time. I'd been in there with Ed for two hours. Then, after another half an hour, Fake-AF Booker came into the office and sat opposite me.

I could tell by the sudden change in atmosphere that it wasn't good news.

'We've all been talking, and I'm afraid it's going to have to be a no,' she said.

I sat there dumbstruck. It felt like I'd been punched in the gut. **WHAT?!**

I did what she said they wanted! I got down to the dream measurements!

'But . . . but . . . you said . . .'

'I know,' she replied. 'But you didn't get down to the size quickly enough. And then there's the height problem . . .' She paused. 'But good luck with other agencies.'

I was absolutely crushed. It wasn't like I'd shrunk in height in the seven weeks she'd last seen me, was it? I'd given up two months to lose this weight, and for what? Fake-AF Booker continued to chew her gum loudly and began chatting to Ed like none of this had ever happened, as though I wasn't in the room. It was like they'd decided not to buy a car because it had the wrong parts.

That night, I ordered the biggest portion of Domino's ever. I'd forgotten how good pizza tasted.

The Brain Deviant didn't let me enjoy it for long.

9

THE ART OF ACTING SANE

Guess what, everyone? Over time, I became normal! Well, from the outside anyway. From the outside, you would've thought I was like everybody else. I blended in, and you'd never, ever, *ever* think I was an obsessive compulsive, anxious weirdo with strange eating rituals.

Yes, I did it! From the outside, my life appeared picture-perfect. But what did 'normal' mean, exactly? I still hadn't entirely worked it out. I could only assume it meant being *happy*, and if there was anything I wanted in this world, it was happiness. I guessed I'd have to fake it till I made it.

I'd stopped chasing modelling, outwardly at least, and my weight was now healthy and normal. I'd started a fashion course at university in London, because that's what normal people did, wasn't it? Go to uni, even if they didn't have much interest in a particular subject. Deep down, I'd never been the clubbing or drinking type, but normal people liked doing that, didn't they? So that's what I did –

got drunk in rubbish clubs among gross men, pretending I was having a whale of a time, when I would've actually preferred watching a DVD in bed.

Was this what 'normal' was? Boyfriends? Girlfriends? Uni? Money? Holidays? Drunken nights out? If it meant I'd finally be at peace with myself, I wanted these things, too – even if they hadn't appealed to me much before. No matter how many times I applied to agencies, the constant rejection proved my modelling aspirations were becoming more and more unlikely. Perhaps I was searching for happiness in the wrong place?

If people assumed I was happy via the images I posted online, that must've meant I was normal. Right? Wrong!

This is probably the time to tell you how misleading social media is. I know everyone tells you that, and I also know that we all manipulate what we choose to post or not to post on our pages. I mean, we don't choose to post stuff that makes us look bad or ugly, do we? And even though I know I behave this way myself, I still manage to forget that other people do this, too. Their lives aren't as jazzy as they make out, no matter how often they post a photo of their new car or write 'OFF TO MAGALUF WITH DA LADZ'. Their lives may look normal and happy from the outside, but no one's life is perfect. However, when you see a constant array of smiley faces and seemingly perfect lives plastered on a screen in the palm of your hand, we all have a habit of forgetting this fact.

I didn't think about this at the time. I thought I was still the odd one out, that I was the only one who didn't feel 'right' or who didn't have it together. I didn't want my Facebook friends to know that though, obviously. It wasn't like I was going to post a status saying, '*WHAT THE HELL AM I DOING WITH MY LIFE?!*' or, '*Guess what, everyone! I'm so stressed out that I've made myself sick twice today!*' or, '*Shame I only have fifty pounds in my bank account – LOL!*' No. No, of course I didn't. Well, would you? In order to keep up with the Joneses, I had to pretend my life was as hunky-dory as theirs.

Despite the fact that the Brain Deviant had repeatedly told me there wasn't a hope in hell I'd ever get into the London College of Fashion, guess what? I *did* get in. I'd set my mind to it, and I actually did it. For the first time in a billion years my mum and dad were thrilled with me.

I made a great group of friends there. I was very lucky in that respect. Unlike school, where you're kind of thrust into an environment where people may or may not share your ideals, we all bonded over our mutual love of fashion. I bleached my hair bright blonde and got some more random piercings – anything went in fashion school. I had two tongue piercings at one point, cos why not? It didn't suppress my appetite like it had last time, but it did for about four days. Four days without eating gave me a bit more control.

After my experience with the 800-calorie diet, and as I'd expected, I had gained the weight back and more. No one can sustain a diet like that forever. But you know what? After a while, I didn't care. My latest buzz was far greater than how I felt when the number dropped on the scale. It was called HAPPINESS.

I was struggling with the womenswear course, but that didn't matter. I had such a great friendship group that it more than made up for it. But, boy, was I struggling. Womenswear and pattern cutting was all numbers and measurements, neither of which have ever been my strong point except for when it came to counting calories. I mean, I'd cheered and ripped up my book on the day I finished my GCSE maths exam because I was that excited, and my maths teacher had put me in detention afterwards. For one, no one had told me how pricey the course would be. Fashion courses, especially design-based ones, become so expensive, especially once you buy the right tools and fabric. The workload was phenomenal – not an easy ride at all like I'd somewhat hoped. I'd heard about kids partying at uni, but by the time I got home from a day of working I was physically exhausted.

I began paying people in my class to finish my work for me – there were no rules against this, and, besides, some of the rich overseas students openly got their clothes made.

I secretly wished I'd listened to my gut and not gone to uni, but this was a few years ago, and if you didn't go to uni you were basically considered being a stone's throw away from an ASBO. Anyway, no one needed to know I was struggling as much as I was. My confidence was gradually improving, and I am convinced that was down to the fact I no longer put all my emphasis on my looks.

I ignored the itch underneath my skin that told me I craved something more. For the first time in a long time I was making people proud. I finally felt like I was on the right path. I was no longer the misfit I was always made out to be.

I was midway through my second term of uni when I fainted in Tesco. Right by the dairy aisle, to be exact, which wasn't exactly a highlight of my university days. I'd had a bit of a sore throat for a few hours and had popped down to get some orange juice when *BAM!* – I woke up in the storage bit at the back, where they keep all the cardboard boxes and supplies. Usually I would've screamed if I woke up to the sight of four confused men crowded over me, but this time I was too weak.

They'd called an ambulance and it was on its way. Despite trying to convince the paramedic that, no, I was not pregnant, and that, yes, I really did feel fine, they drove me to the hospital. All of a sudden, my throat felt like it was on fire. Never had I experienced this sort of pain. What made it worse was that I was totally on my own, needing a hug. I sat in A & E for hours and almost fainted from the pain again, until six hours later I was sent home diagnosed with a severe case of tonsillitis and a ton of codeine to get me through it.

Over the next couple of weeks, I dropped over a stone in weight. I was still eating the same, but now I was less than eight stone and the physical changes were quite drastic. I had cheekbones, for one.

People began doing double takes when I'd walk into a lecture, or, even worse, would tell me how great I looked. I would smile through gritted teeth while I tried not to fall asleep through the mist of codeine, a powerful painkiller. I'd fall asleep on the Tube or in lectures because of how relaxed I was. But most of all, I was calm: calmer than I'd ever been. It made me forget about the Year We Do Not Talk About and the evil ex-boyfriend. None of my problems mattered any more. My course didn't matter any more. Best of all, like class-A drugs, it suppressed my appetite. I now only ate when I felt I needed to. I was hooked.

Rather than being concerned about my continual weight loss, however, I BLOODY LOVED IT. I was thinner than I'd ever been. Even once my tonsillitis cleared, the weight was dropping off. What a dream!

Now, a sane person would view this extreme weight loss as something serious, which it undeniably was. But not me. I revelled in the attention I was getting. Friends and lecturers would approach me concerned, and other girls told me enviously how they wished they could have my figure, which is kind of messed up, if you think about it. I guess I wasn't entirely over my eating disorder, no matter how much I liked to pretend otherwise. It had always been lurking, and now it was back with a vengeance. And so, like a broken record, the modelling question popped up again.

Because I was now underweight, I was approached by a few older students to model their fashion collections. I did it for a bit of extra cash, letting them drape their designs over my frail frame. I began getting scouted by agencies again, only for them to – you've guessed it – never actually sign me. It now wasn't the weight issue, but the height problem instead.

One day, I walked into my university canteen when I bumped into an old male model friend of mine doing a graduate fashion-week casting. I'd known him since we were about sixteen, and he'd always believed in me. He'd always encouraged me to keep going where modelling was concerned and genuinely believed I was model material.

I couldn't help but feel somewhat envious of the models standing around me. They were tall, they were glamorous, they were beautiful. They were also swanning around London while I was failing (and fainting) at university, the lucky gits.

'You gonna give modelling another try then?' he asked.

'Are you joking?' I replied, scoffing. I looked nothing like these glamazons, and was kidding myself if I ever thought I would.

'Have a think about it,' he said. 'I'm not gonna lie – you are a bit short –' FYI I am 5 foot 8 inches – 'but why don't you keep going to agencies and see what happens?'

I promised him I'd think about it, but no longer had the courage. I didn't want to get let down again.

It is during an attempt to appear like 'one of the girls' that I meet my first normal adult boyfriend, Scott – in a dodgy nightclub in Berlin with some friends, to the sounds of German techno music billowing away in the background, and just after I'd threatened to punch a drunk guy who'd randomly kissed me on the mouth.

Scott came from an incredibly normal background and was nine and a half years older than me. He seemed so grown-up and worldly-wise, full of facts and knowledge. Unlike me, he'd lived in the same house his entire life – I'd lost count of how many places I'd lived in by this point. He was still friends with the people he'd been to school and university with; I'd lost touch with most of mine. It transpired that Scott and I were living in the same area of London, and that felt normal, dating someone who lived nearby and who knew all the same spots as me. In my mind, anyone who had a successful, solid relationship dated local people.

I was drawn to the fact he was comforting and safe; Scott was drawn to the fact my life seemed exciting and cultural and a bit all over the place. Once we were back on British soil, he took me to London's Brick Lane for some bagels, and that was it – I got myself a boyfriend. One who wasn't an abusive dick, which made a nice change.

The only un-normal thing about Scott's life was his brief stint as a musician, when he'd been signed to a major record label with moderate success. Funnily enough, I'd seen him and his band play when I was fifteen – I'd got bruises on my hips from rowdy drunk men pushing me into the metal gates at the front of the stage, and I could've sworn that I'd had my drink spiked that night at the after party, but that's as much as I recall. Scott would go on and on and *on* about the 'good old days' he'd had when he was touring, and I'd listen intently, fascinated by the fact that I was going out with someone whose life seemed so rock 'n' roll.

Whenever I'm happy or relaxed, it's as though my eating disorder vanishes into thin air. When I first met Scott my disordered eating still lurked in the background – making me count calories and obsessively calculate my daily allowance – but as I fell deeper in love with him and we kept going on dates to restaurants and cafes like normal couples, worrying about food was no longer my main concern. For the first time in a long time, my eating disorder was on hold.

Scott was a dreamer. His head was in the clouds, and every day he'd tell me all the things he was going to do in the future, like the exotic countries he'd visit and vintage cars he'd buy. And I, being the awestruck nineteen-year-old I was, became wrapped up in these stories, clinging on to every dream of his as though it was my own.

Eventually, I'd push all my aspirations to the side for his. I'd repeatedly tell him what he wanted to hear – that he was going to be successful and rich – and he'd lap it up. Who cared about my dreams, eh?! My life was about living for his! His dreams and how he spoke so confidently about his future comforted me, making me feel less anxious about the uncertainties of my own.

I began distancing myself from my own friends in favour of his. I don't need to tell you this was a silly idea, but I couldn't bear to be away from Scott. Gone were days out with friends or going out to a bar or two. My life became

Scott, Scott, Scott, and I was utterly addicted to being with him.

While I have a tendency to be overdramatic with these kinds of things, going on the pill was HELL for my skin.

Everyone is different, but within a month of taking it, my face was covered in huge red cysts. I'd had oily skin as a teenager, yes, but nothing like this sh*t heap. It was like a skin monster had taken over my entire body and turned me into a human version of a pepperoni pizza.

While it's important to stay safe, contraception and me don't mix. But I was nineteen, in my first 'proper' relationship, and going on the pill was just what you did, wasn't it? Staying safe and baby-free is never a boy's problem . . . right? Right?!

Well, in the end, this severe reaction I was having became everyone's problem. My mood swings were more up and down than my cheating ex's boxers, yet my GP (who was terrible, by the way) told me to keep going with it. 'This is just a normal side effect,' he insisted, though my gut said otherwise.

So I continued to gain weight and deal with the painful skin. I remember accidentally brushing my face with a hairbrush once and crying out in pain. It was excruciating. And now not only was I broke and scared about my future, but also more insecure than I'd ever been about my looks.

A year before I met him, Scott had been working on a solo record. This, he said, was a masterpiece – better than any of his old band's stuff. This album would be legendary. But producing this record had also left him broke. He had no money to call his own. As a thirty-year-old, he was still living at home with his very traditional parents, working on new songs on a computer in a spare room at the top of the house.

As I continued to struggle at uni, something magical happened. Scott was offered another recording contract with one of the world's biggest labels for £50,000. Can you imagine?! I couldn't – money like that was in my dreams. I was still living off my university loan, lending Scott money whenever he needed it and paying for meals out just so it felt like we were having a *normal* dating experience. But this was only the start of an amazing future together, I was sure of it! Imagine that – little old me, with a famous musician boyfriend.

By this stage, we'd been dating a good two years. I paid for it all – meals, days out, petrol for *his* car. I had a part-time receptionist job at a hairdresser's on Saturday mornings, but got fired from that after accidentally playing some very expletive-laden Kanye West songs and scaring an old lady having a perm (bit of an overreaction, if I do say so myself). I'd then got a part-time job in a pub, but Scott got me fired after threatening my boss, accusing him of coming on to me. I was bored of staying in south-east London, when my university friends were sunning around in the south of France. I was a sugar mama, but a twenty-one-year-old one looking after a now-thirty-one-year-old.

Eventually, I couldn't afford to take us out any more. I was SKINT. I began to feel envious of girls being spoiled by their boyfriends, who got flowers or treats on the odd occasion. But when I'd get annoyed at Scott for not pulling his weight or not getting a part-time job, he'd tell me we didn't need money: that our love conquered all. He had a great way of romanticizing situations, or making me feel bad for wanting what normal girls had. Besides, when he was rich and famous, he'd spoil me for eternity.

As time went on, Scott became increasingly impossible to live with.

It started off with cooking. He had to be in control of each and every mealtime, asking me to leave him alone in the kitchen. At first, I thought this was Scott's way of making up for his lack of money – cooking me dinners as a way of showing he cared. And don't get me wrong: he was a very good chef. But every meal would take up to an hour or so to make, sometimes even longer. Then I'd wash the dishes in two minutes and put them away. But Scott would take them out of the cupboard and inspect them rigorously. My efforts were never good enough, and he'd always redo them.

The record label's promises of paying Scott his money in one month turned into two, then three, then six months, and before you knew it, they hadn't paid him it in a year. Understandably, because the money from the advance wasn't coming through, this stressed him out even more. And so he'd become more and more agitated. The slightest thing caused an argument.

When he did eventually get that advance money, guess what? He blew it in around six months. This, apparently, was all my fault. He'd allegedly lost fifty grand by taking me out for a meal once or twice a week, even though he *always* insisted he pay for it all, and also despite the fact the first two years of our relationship were entirely paid for by me. He blamed me for blowing the money on the expensive designer handbag he'd bought me for Christmas, even though he'd surprised me with it.

Now, I'm sure you're reading this and going, 'Here you go! Another bad boyfriend! Why didn't you just dump him?!' But I didn't view him that way. Compared to the awful men I'd dated before, Scott seemed like an angel.

If it hadn't been noticeable that womenswear fashion design was not my forte, the fact that I failed my course said it all. Well, I failed when I first handed in my final coursework; I had the summer to correct it until I passed, and even *then* I only passed by the skin of my teeth.

Going to the London College of Fashion had provided a great distraction from agonizing over what to do in the real world. As the end of my course approached, I knew I had to get a job . . . but doing what? My degree was so specific that I was finding it hard to get hired anywhere.

So now I was twenty-one, had graduated from uni a good three months prior, without any career prospects and a degree that I didn't know what to do with. Great! I applied to restaurants, to bars – even to bloody McDonald's – to no avail. I think it's safe to say you've hit a low point when an employer thinks you're not capable of serving a few chicken nuggets and milkshakes.

There was no other option than to go on the dole and go to the Job Centre every week. What a total failure I'd become. I'd wanted to prove all my doubters wrong, and here I was, signing on in bloody Peckham. I knew I wanted to do well in life, becoming an Independent Woman à la Destiny's Child, and yet this looked like it would never, ever happen.

But life is full of ups and downs. There's a theory that for every bad thing that happens to you in life, something equally as great will happen. And after months of being depressed AF, this is what happened to me.

I remember the evening clearly. I had just been to Sainsbury's and didn't have a scrap of make-up on. I'd given up caring about my appearance by this point, because it seemed as though my acne was never going to improve. It was an autumn night and already dark by this point, pouring with rain. To add to my luck, I'd forgotten an umbrella and was sitting on my own underneath a flickering light at a bus stop in south-east London.

Five minutes passed, then ten. No buses had come. I began worrying about how much I'd spent food shopping. Could I afford next week's food shop? And then, all of a sudden, I began to cry. God, I was capable of so much more than this! As my school friends were progressing, here I was, crying at a bus stop because there was no escape from my situation.

Then, as though it was a scene in a film, my phone began to ring. It was the male model I'd bumped into at uni a few months previously. He'd since quit to become a scout, bringing potential models to agencies where he'd make a fee for finding them if they were signed.

Argh, not now, I thought to myself, but he wouldn't stop ringing. I wiped my tears and quickly put the phone to my ear inside my hoodie so as not to get rain on it.

'I hope you don't mind,' he said, which meant I probably would mind, 'but I've sent your Facebook photos off to some agencies. And guess what – they want to meet you!'

'My Facebook photos?! Which agencies?' I replied.

He reeled them off. Three huge ones in London wanted to meet me, including the one that had turned me down when I'd starved myself for months.

'But I've been to see all of them before,' I said. 'They've all turned me down at least twice.'

'Well, now they're all interested in signing you,' he said.

And then I remembered something else.

'What about my skin?!'

'I already told them about it, and they don't care. You can work on it. It's only temporary. Stop worrying.'

I didn't want to get my hopes up. I'd been let down too many times by this stage to fall for false hopes. But something told me this time was different.

'So – when are you free to meet them?'

10

MY UN-FAIRY-TALE ENDING

My dream came true.

I was signed on the understanding that I would get my hip span down from thirty-seven inches to thirty-five–thirty-four in a dream scenario. Easy, right? The other agencies I'd visited said they'd only sign me if I got down to the magical thirty-four mark. Thirty-five seemed doable.

Except it wasn't 'doable' at all. No matter how much I cut out foods or watched my weight, the magic number was still out of reach. Before long, the Brain Deviant began to rear its ugly head again, telling me I wasn't doing enough, that I was fat and useless. I was doing everything right – eating more healthily, exercising a bit more – and yet nothing on the measuring tape changed. So I began to keep an even closer eye, desperate to be model material at last.

Getting signed to a modelling agency was supposed to change my life. It was supposed to make up for the years of insecurities and body image issues, and the feeling that I never truly belonged. I was meant to be perfect, yet I didn't *feel* perfect in the slightest. Modelling was supposed to make me happy . . . so why the hell wasn't I?

It didn't make any sense. I truly believed that once the ink on the contract was dry, that was it: my life would be complete and I'd be in control. And, if anything, my life was spiralling downwards.

The agents were excited about me at first. I was fresh meat, after all. The agency director took me under her wing. She'd discovered some of the most famous super-models around, so to have her as an agent felt like a dream come true. I was told point-blank that I'd never do runway modelling because of my height, but that wasn't deemed a problem. The only issue was that because I was so short I allegedly needed to look thinner to 'balance it out' and to *look* like a runway girl.

They'd send me copies of my latest photos by email, writing, *LOOK HOW GREAT YOU LOOK! :)*, and I'd feel elated for a bit, pleased that a few of my photos had made them happy. But somehow the happiness never lasted, and would dwindle after an hour or so until I felt low again.

Everything I thought about modelling until that point was wrong, and anyone who says it's an easy profession doesn't have a bloody clue. People think you get rich from standing in front of a camera every now and then. But you think you get paid for every shoot? Yeah, right! You're expected to do a lot of test shoots for your book for free in the hope that they will lead to gigs, and even then getting paid work isn't guaranteed. So many girls get dropped if they don't book anything. Before you've even made a penny, you're having to reach into your own pocket and find the funds to pay for your portfolio and cards, travelling to and from shoots, buying clothes to wear to castings or for gym memberships.

Modelling is impossible to plan your life around, because it *becomes* your life. You tend to find out your schedule the night before, so it makes it difficult to book appointments or have a spontaneous day out. This includes weekends. You can't wake up one day and think, *I'm going to relax on the diet today*, because you never know what casting or job you might have tomorrow – if you get one. You don't work or go on castings every day. You may have seven days of back-to-back castings or shoots, and then not have a single thing for a month. And you have to be comfortable with that.

So you can imagine how the uncertainty isn't particularly helpful to someone with anxiety – someone who is terrified of what could potentially go wrong 24/7. While nobody knows what may or may not happen in the future, with hard work in a normal profession there is a progression: a pay rise, or chance of a promotion. Promotions don't exist in the modelling world. You either become well known and make more money, or you don't.

Modelling is a game based entirely on luck. It's all about being in the right place at the right time, having the facial features that happen to be fashionable right now, or knowing the right people. There's no 'climbing up the career ladder' – you either make it, or you don't. Your career essentially lies in your agent's hands – there's only so much you can manipulate on your own – and they'll dictate which casting directors you'll see, which magazines you're sent to or which photographers you'll shoot with. And not everyone becomes the next Kate Moss. There are plenty of girls making hundreds of thousands shooting e-comm work – you know, the girls you see on clothing websites – who will never become household names.

You've got to have a persona on social media, too, or at least do something interesting on the side. You have to have something that makes you stand out from the crowd, like – I don't know – being an undertaker or something equally bizarre. Like aspiring actresses or singers, you're a dime a dozen. Becoming a well-known model is nigh on impossible, and even if you do 'make it' in the fashion industry, there's no guarantee any regular person is going to recognize you or ask for your autograph. Does becoming famous indicate your success?

I know I sound like I'm moaning. So why didn't I just quit? Because when modelling goes well it's WONDER-FUL. Seriously, it's everything you imagined it could be and more: glamorous, exciting, dramatic. These bits are what you don't want to let go of. You meet the most creative and interesting people, who, like me, once dreamt of breaking into the fashion industry. And while you're not curing diseases, you're creating images that allow the average person to escape from the mundanities of everyday life. When it's good, it's the most fabulous job in the world.

Once you've received a big pay cheque, it's very hard to let that go and get a 'normal' job or career. Most fashion people stay for the money because they won't earn that amount anywhere else. Brands will think nothing of dropping huge sums of money on productions – I did a job recently that cost in excess of $500,000 – and who would want to turn down the travelling, hotels and big shoots? The clothes, the parties, the catering, the creative teams of people you work with . . . it's like stepping into the pages of a fairy tale. And I think this was another reason I didn't want to give up modelling: my teenage dreams of what I imagined modelling to be were often realized, and I got to live those dreams.

I wanted to make it work so badly that if I wasn't obsessively watching what I ate, I was obsessively trying to create luck for myself.

You see, if I managed to create luck for myself, perhaps I would be become successful. I began looking for lucky opportunities everywhere. For example, I stopped walking under ladders, because this could affect my luck. I'd cross my fingers if I crossed somebody on the stairs. I'd make a wish at 11:11 to become successful. Somebody told me it was unlucky to drink alcohol without looking at someone in the eye first, or if you clinked an alcoholic and non-alcoholic drink together. I'd read my horoscope religiously until I read something positive. I'd salute two magpies for 'joy' (like in the poem, 'One for sorrow, two for joy'), and would go mad if I couldn't find another magpie if I'd seen just the one. I may not have had much control over how my career would pan out, but I could try to assume some control over how lucky I'd be.

I never knew what I'd be getting when I went into the agency. It became a game of Mood Roulette, where you'd never know what vibe you'd be confronted with.

I'd go in one day and the bookers would appear calm and happy – God forbid, *friendly*, almost – and I'd chuckle to myself, wondering what I'd ever been so nervous about. *It's all in your head!* I'd think. But then the next time I visited, I'd snappily be asked why I wasn't toned enough yet, or why I wasn't taking the job seriously, when in reality I'd never taken anything more seriously in my entire life.

When I went into the agency I'd be met by a group of skinny, glamorous people eyeing me up and down. Sometimes they couldn't be bothered to greet me at all – physically unable, it seemed, to mutter a courteous 'hello'. In the end I realized that if they studied me and didn't say anything, nice or not, I was fine. *Phew!* But I was constantly waiting for the next bout of catty comments.

It wasn't just me; they weren't particularly nice to each other, either. I'd sit there uncomfortably while the intern was being yelled at, or look down at my lap when she stepped outside crying. I'd listen to them laughing nastily about a girl who'd just walked in, or talking about who they were going to drop. How did I know I wouldn't be next?

And so I lived with the idea that one day my agents would come to their senses and drop me . . . because why wouldn't they? I couldn't understand how, despite my millions of flaws, I was still on their books. I was desperate to remain a model, and even though deep down I knew I wasn't that happy, I pushed that fact to the back of my mind. I was constantly living for the 'We're sorry, but . . .' discussion . . . And this wait for what I believed to be inevitable kept me constantly on edge.

Needless to say, this uncertainty was the perfect recipe for my eating disorders to completely take over my life again.

I wasn't the only new model on the board when I joined. The agency was growing rapidly, representing some of fashion's best new faces, and it was comforting to have a friendly group of girls from around the world to share that with.

I suggested that a group of us go on a trip to Nando's as a chance to bond. It was affordable, it was convenient, and who doesn't like a cheeky Nando's on a Friday night?

I'll tell you who: a bunch of models.

We were all *ooh*-ing and *aah*-ing at what to order from the menu – not because Nando's is renowned for its variety of food options, but because we were all worried about what a chicken wing would do to our physiques. I pretended to glance at the menu like I was seeing it for the first time, but I'd already googled the calories of a piri-piri chicken pita beforehand, and I'm pretty sure these girls had, too.

Aside from the fact we were starving ourselves as a social activity, the meal went really well. After breaking the ice over, quite literally, water and ice, people began discussing the individual pressures they'd faced from our team of bookers.

All of us had been told to lose weight – including the 5-foot-11-inch girl who was a size zero, and the girl who could have been a Victoria's Secret model – in fact, she was so beautiful that she did model for them eventually. No one was spared the harsh comments. It appeared that no matter how much money you made, or however beautiful you were, you were not exempt from criticism.

It also transpired that all six of us were terrified of going into the agency alone. I wasn't the only one whose legs turned to jelly or who felt physically sick before I'd even arrived. This news made me feel slightly more sane – it wasn't my insecurity speaking; other people felt the same. All of us were made to feel victimized or uncomfortable, whether it was being told to lose weight we didn't have, or instructed to buy expensive handbags so that it appeared we were more well off and successful than we actually were, or told to change something about our hair/make-up/clothes every week. And so we made a vow that we would try to go in in pairs or as a group to support each other, and to help make the experience less nerve-wracking.

I couldn't possibly risk going over my daily calorie allowance, which was now a mere 1,100 calories a day or less. How I came up with that number I don't know, but in OCD-terms it just felt 'right': 1,100 calories was 'healthy' to me. It was more than I'd eaten when I'd first starved myself in a bid for a modelling career, so it must've been OK. Right?

I stopped going out for social occasions. I became a total recluse, keeping myself to myself. People just wouldn't 'get' my absurd diet, or understand what I was going through, assuming I was being difficult. I knew they thought I was crazy, because I was. Besides, the Brain Deviant told me I'd be a nuisance and annoy them.

By dinner, I'd usually be left with 200–300 calories. I'd feel shaky and wobbly, my hands trembling and my mood irritable or snappy, but nothing could prepare people for the wrath they'd face if I went over that calorie allowance. Half of me knew I was being neurotic; the other half refused to relinquish any form of control. I would measure foods and sauces perfectly, googling the exact calorie amount in a spoonful or cup of something and rounding it up to the nearest whole number so as not to go over my calories for the day.

Scott tried to be as sympathetic as possible to my situation at first. Like most, he didn't see this as an eating disorder – rather, someone just being difficult. Despite me being a pain, he'd plan meals around me and my very specific diet, making sure we ate 'healthily' (i.e. gluten free, low carb, no dairy – despite the fact that we were allergic to zero of them). Recently, he'd also got into healthy eating, so this worked out perfectly. Around 4 p.m. every day, my blood-sugar levels would drop, so I'd eat two or three extra-sugary penny sweets to get me through to dinner. Scott would call me immature for having sweets in the drawer. 'What are you – a kid?' he'd say. 'No one should eat them past the age of twelve.'

I'd categorically refuse to eat a meal if Scott sprinkled an ounce of salt on top of the food. If I could taste it, I would go mental, getting tearful and angry, like he was deliberately trying to sabotage my career. I know that makes me sound ungrateful and mean, but I was a woman possessed. More correctly, I was ill. Well and truly mentally ill.

Food containing gluten would send me over the edge. Because I had cut it out completely, it would leave me with severe stomach pains if I ate it. I'd read all the ingredients on packets of food, seeing if they contained gluten. Do you know how many foods it's in – let alone dressings?! Well, if you're an anorexic, you'll know.

'ARE YOU TRYING TO RUIN MY LIFE?!' I'd scream, and he'd start yelling back, saying how modelling was spoiling everything – which it was, though I wouldn't admit it. I couldn't remember the last time I'd been happy. Food was so unenjoyable, and yet, as it had at so many other times, it completely dictated my life.

At the time I thought I was doing a great job at masking my anxiety, which had gradually got worse and worse, but my nervousness couldn't have been more obvious. Whenever I went to my agency or to castings I was plastered in tiny, glistening beads of sweat. *What will they say to me today? What will I end up obsessing over until I see them again?*

Polaroids were the worst. They're physical photos taken on a digital camera to send to clients and show them what you really look like, without Photoshop. I'd stand there, shaking in my underwear while sucking in my tummy, thinking of how morbidly obese I must look and what a let-down I was.

'Your body is fine for a normal girl's, but for modelling . . . they like *thin*,' my agent once said, like she was doing me a favour. I didn't want to hear the words 'normal' or 'healthy'. I didn't want to look healthy. I wanted to look *thin* and elite, like the rest of the girls.

Polaroids became an excuse to berate me even further, to tell me how my hair needed to be changed, or how my clothes were bad, or how disappointing it was that my skin had flared up again.

Oh yes, my skin. How could I forget that?! It had been improving bit by bit, but recently it was slowly getting worse again. Perhaps it was down to how nervous I constantly was, or the low-calorie diet I was on, but my skin felt like it was bubbling beneath the surface: itchy and sensitive and raw. I downed litres of water. I didn't eat junk food. I'd cut out dairy. I wasn't on any hormonal contraceptives. And yet it was getting worse, all along my jawline, which is where hormonal acne shows up on your face.

Anxiety sent my hormones into overdrive, as did my low-calorie diet. I'd survive on caffeine to stay awake and this would make my anxiety worse. My mind would start spinning, my heart pounding, and I'd start worrying about being dropped, or what the agents would be saying about me behind my back, or thinking about how skint I was (which, by the way, was very. I made no money at all). The low-calorie diet was screwing up my body – I knew this because my periods were so infrequent – but I didn't care because this meant I was losing weight. And because my hormones were so all over the place my skin would flare up again.

Weirdly, if I had a 'bad day' – which, to me, consisted of eating in the region of 1,500 calories – my skin would improve drastically overnight. Spots would disappear almost instantly. I knew my diet was destroying my skin, but I cared so much about my weight that I would've rather looked like a pepperoni pizza for the rest of my life if it meant being size zero.

And so I kept dieting and trying to reach this unattainable size, because no matter how many times my agents picked something wrong with me, I was desperate to hear the words, 'You're perfect.'

But they never came, because perfection doesn't exist.

Meanwhile, Scott and I were now arguing every day.

We were driving each other mad. My eating disorder made me impossible to live with, and his ridiculously high standards for tidiness didn't help.

I did try my best to tidy up, but my attempts were never good enough for Scott, as though we were living at The Ritz. If a glass had a water stain on it, I'd get a lecture on how I disrespected the place, or didn't take pride in how I lived. I was so anxious all day (if I even had a job that day), and home was just as stressful. At least it distracted me from admitting that I had a problem.

Mental health issues do NOT improve when one is surrounded by arseholes, and there were plenty of those people in the fashion industry. As a model, you learn to appreciate that not everyone likes your face or 'gets' you, including some of the agents. But there was one particular guy who made me, and tons of other girls, squirm, relishing the fact he could juggle your career in the palm of his hand.

There were so many men like this – so why didn't we tell them where to go? Well, it was difficult. These idiots often had the power to mould your career or push it in a certain direction. With a thirty-five-inch hip, I still didn't feel like 'model material'. Ever heard of the phrase 'Don't bite the hand that feeds you'? I may not have bitten a chunk of their hands off (can you imagine the calorie content?!), but considering these people favouritized girls they wanted to send to the top castings, I didn't want to ruin any chance I had of making it. So, like a coward, I kept quiet, eagerly trying to please them.

One of the worst offenders was often in our agency, so just like we'd agreed in Nando's, we kept our promise of trying to go into the agency in pairs or as a group. Someone set up a Facebook thread, and we would message each other to see if someone else could come in with us on the day we were needed. We would make an excuse about why we also happened to be in the area, like, 'Oh! I've run out of cards and need some new ones,' or, 'Can I see what my schedule is like?' Honestly, it softened the blow.

My comments were always, *always* about my weight.

My bookers wouldn't outwardly say, 'You need to lose a stone' or, 'You're too fat,' because that's a lawsuit waiting to happen. I began noticing that they never, ever wrote those comments down in an email; it was conveniently said on the phone or in person. They'd make out like they wanted to help me; that they wanted me to look 'the best I could'.

Oh, f***ing do one. I was a size six, for God's sake.

They'd say things like, 'Those inches will come off if you go to the gym more,' or, 'You're a model; you're meant to be the person all girls want to be, with the body all girls want to have,' or, 'I'm going on a diet now, actually – why don't we embark on one together, ha ha?!' But losing weight when you're already thin is easier said than done.

In fact, these agents probably knew perfectly well that an already slim person cannot lose inches as easily as that. You're not going to lose three inches in a month, not unless you're clinically obese. So they kind of expect you to read between the lines and come up with another way of making the weight drop. Besides, if you don't get rid of it, there are plenty of girls ready and willing to take your place.

Once, I was told to only eat vegetables for breakfast, lunch and dinner. 'By all means eat, but just make sure it's vegetables! They'll keep you fuller for longer.' So I did, and, rather unsurprisingly, quickly became bored (not to mention moody) following this bizarre diet.

I'm sure you can guess what happens when you try to lose weight and it doesn't work the way you'd like. You begin to hate yourself even more. You hate your body for not being able to morph itself into other models' bodies, who seem to make the whole thing seem so effortless. You forget that all bodies hold weight differently, that not one body in the world is the same as another. You beat yourself up over something you can't control. You try desperately to be someone else.

Yet agents, who as far as you're aware hold the key to your dreams, tell you it is possible. 'It's only a couple of inches!' they repeatedly say, holding their fingers apart to show just how easy it allegedly is. 'That's it!'

And they're right. That's it. A measly couple of inches. A couple of inches, and then your dreams are in reach. I'd heard it long enough – 'We'll send you to see [insert top brand/designer/casting director here] once you get your hips down. They won't see you otherwise.' But no matter what diet plan you follow, it just doesn't come off. You may be able to lose weight, but you can't lose bone.

One agent told me to do squats to lose the inches. And so I did. I did around 150 to 200 squats a day until the backs of my thighs felt like they were on fire. I did this for months. But when I measured myself the number on the tape was going up, not down. Huh?! My bum looked toned and Kardashian-worthy, better than it ever had, but it wasn't thin. It was disgusting. Beauty was measured by a number, and a peachy bum was not beautiful. Curves were repulsive.

I began to run instead. Despite the fact I had no energy from lack of food, I ran until my legs turned to jelly and my head pounded. I had to go for a run first thing in the morning, because just after waking up was the only time I'd have energy to get up and do it. Aside from attending the odd casting, I'd have absolutely no energy to leave the house in the afternoons, let alone run. Once I'd run a few miles, I'd have no energy for the rest of the day, so the majority of my afternoons were spent watching things like *Jeremy Kyle* or *Homes Under the Hammer*. What a glamorous life!

You may think sitting at home doing absolutely nothing is a dream. It might be, for a couple of weeks, but gradually you start going brain-dead. This is what happened to me. I was slowly beginning to lose my mind and sense of purpose. My life revolved around mealtimes or runs. I'd refresh my emails constantly, partly hoping an email from my agency would come in, while also hoping it didn't. I was starting to dread anything modelling related.

Not only that, but my mind was genuinely starting to go. I was becoming forgetful. I'd go into the kitchen and forget why I'd gone in, or would put my phone in the fridge by accident, or would have to stop talking midway through a sentence because I couldn't remember what I was talking about. It didn't frighten me to start with, but it did begin to happen more and more frequently. I don't know if this was down to not eating properly, or down to not using my brain, but I'm sure it was a bit of both. Humans are designed to have a sense of purpose, and yet I was so hell-bent on becoming a model that I began to forget I had other things to offer – other things that made me a good, interesting person.

Scott would find this frustrating when he got home in the evenings, and ask why I hadn't done anything all day, and I wanted to explain that I physically couldn't – that I was too weak – but the words wouldn't come out. It was like an invisible force (cough, the Brain Deviant, cough) was stopping me from speaking. Besides, I knew he'd tell me to stop modelling, and I didn't want him to lecture me on that yet again. Even walking upstairs to the bathroom would leave me breathless, my heart palpitating, and I'd have to take a minute to breathe and hold myself steady in case I fell over. Admitting I was too tired and weak was like admitting I wasn't model material, and I couldn't possibly let him know that I was struggling.

Running, I assumed, would get the weight off. But it didn't. I was running five to six miles a day, six days a week, losing my mind with worry and regret if I missed a day. After a while, the weight stalled, or on a particularly 'bad' day (mainly around my period) the measuring tape would say I'd gained inches. How could that be?! I began to panic. They'd drop me from their books, I was sure of it. Despite the fact I was barely working as a model, the last thing I wanted was to let go of my model status. I cared too deeply about modelling for that to happen. Without modelling, I had nothing.

I'd incessantly google things like 'Gaining muscle from running', 'Does muscle make you weigh more?', 'Do squats make your bum bigger or smaller?' and 'Why am I not losing weight?'. If my agent said running and squatting were the key to losing weight, then why the f*ck weren't they working?

Here's why it wasn't working. My body isn't designed to be thin on the bottom. I am a pear shape – I have a smaller upper half and curvier bottom. Not only that, but the people giving me this so-called 'advice' WEREN'T HEALTHCARE PROFESSIONALS. They were people who came out of uni or college, sometimes even school, with barely any knowledge of how their own bodies worked, let alone somebody else's. They weren't original enough to think, *Hey, guess what, we could make a star out of someone who isn't as small as other girls.* No one is going to buy something advertised by a person who weighs a healthy amount, are they?

Or are they? In reality, despite what some high-end fashion houses believe, there's absolutely no correlation between using bigger models (like a size ten/twelve up) and selling fewer products. What I've discovered since then is that women are drawn to pretty women of all different shapes and sizes. Having a size-fourteen woman modelling clothes doesn't put people off buying something, as long as she's photographed in a beautiful, aspirational and high-end way.

But, according to agencies at that time, when girls couldn't lose weight like they expected them to they weren't taking their jobs seriously enough.

In fact, this was said to me one afternoon.

'Do you just not care at all about modelling?' one booker said in reference to my apparent lack of weight loss, and I began to sweat.

'No!' I spluttered. 'No! No, not at all. I want to model more than anything.'

'Well, it doesn't *look* that way,' he said, eyeing my body, and then he returned to his desk, his back turned to me.

The only way the numbers did go down on the measuring tape was if I didn't exercise. Weird, I know, but that was the only way. Want to know why? Because my muscles were physically wasting away and eating themselves. Isn't that an attractive image! But when you crave thinness the way I did, you don't give a damn if your body is eating itself to survive. It's great, if anything. You turn a bit flabbier, but the numbers on the measuring tape are down. You weigh less on the scale because there isn't any muscle – an important part of your body that keeps you healthy and strong. But who cares about being healthy when you can be *thin*?

11

A NIGHTMARE IN PARIS

Knock, knock.

Who's there?

Me.

Me who?

Me, your good old friend anxiety!

Yep, it was back, and with it my bulimia – but this time with a vengeance. If I didn't have enough on my plate to deal with, I was now continually throwing up whatever was on my plate, too.

Numbers, numbers, numbers. My life revolved around them. If I wasn't weighing myself up to ten times a day, I was obsessively measuring myself, desperately hoping my hip span hadn't gone up, typing my daily calorie intake into the calculator on my phone and saving it into a special 'dieting document', or giving myself dates on the calendar to lose weight by.

When I looked in the mirror all I saw was fat. I was eight stone by this point, medically underweight for my height, but this was considered a 'normal' weight in my mind. I wasn't thin enough. The Brain Deviant told me I needed to weigh seven. When I look back at photos I can see how prominent my hip bones and ribcage were, and yet at the time it didn't reflect in the mirror. I was just fat and flaws. I'd grab any squishy bits of my body and wince with embarrassment and shame.

I remember putting on a pair of designer jeans on one shoot for a magazine, which were a UK size eight, and they just fell off me. They were so baggy that the stylist had to clip them from the back.

I didn't get it. The label clearly stated they were a size eight, but when I looked in the mirror I saw the reflection of someone at least three times bigger. It was as though somebody was playing a trick on me. I was beyond confused, yet still felt a rush of excitement through my veins. Losing weight was a thrill far bigger than anything else I'd ever experienced – better than any drug.

If I saw my family and they told me I'd lost weight or that I looked 'too thin', I got my high again, feeling as though I was drifting through the clouds. But if someone said I looked 'well', I lost it. It was a compliment, and yet the walls around me would feel like they were caving in. As far as I was concerned, if I looked well, that meant I looked healthy, and if I looked healthy, that meant I was fat. How's that for logic?

Anorexia and bulimia are cries for help, which is certainly true in my case. I wanted help, I really did, but admitting I had a problem was like admitting I was a failure, that I couldn't keep up with the other models. And believe me – a lot of them had problems, too. They just wouldn't admit it, either.

Even if people thought I had an eating disorder, they certainly didn't say anything. People might've said I looked thin or bony, but I'd take it as a compliment. Even to this day, I still believe that in modelling terms I didn't look thin enough. People saw thin models every day, and I simply wasn't on their level. I was unhealthy, yes, and small for everyday standards, but didn't look malnourished by fashion standards then. I may have had a lollipop head, but my body didn't *shock*.

I wanted to be saved from the demons inside my head. But the words just wouldn't come out. Why was nobody listening? Why could nobody see how lonely I was? Perhaps by dieting further, my body would look frail and small, and my body would speak for itself. Maybe they'd finally see how fragile I felt inside.

'Your body is really holding you back,' I was told in a meeting one day, very matter-of-factly. My heart dropped. It was the first time anyone had directly told me what I felt deep down to be true. Every negative thing I thought about myself when I looked at my reflection was clearly not a lie. 'I can't send your pictures to clients looking like this, Charli.'

'*You failure!*' the Brain Deviant screamed.

I looked down at my lap feeling absolutely mortified, as other bookers listened nearby. I knew they had a point. I may have been a UK size six/eight but I clearly wasn't doing enough. I was trying to exercise or leave the house as much as possible, but it's hard when you have zero energy to do anything. A two-minute trip to the local shop felt like a mission in itself, let alone a walk around Tesco. I was getting excruciating knife-like cramps in the arches and soles of my feet that made it difficult to stand.

'You always look so tired,' another booker chipped in. 'Whenever I see you, there are dark circles under your eyes.' This wasn't new. I'd been paranoid about this since receiving a couple of emails from people at the agency telling me how tired I looked, and how I needed to rest. But with barely any work offers or castings, all I seemed to be doing was resting. I could sleep and sleep for hours, sometimes twelve hours or more, and the skin around my eyes would still look puffy and dull when I woke up. I'd got into the habit of holding frozen packets of peas on my eyelids every morning in an attempt to wake me up a bit, to no avail. In fact, I couldn't remember the last time I had truly felt energized or capable of doing anything. 'I think you should get tested for your iron levels.'

My iron levels? I'd never had any problems with them before.

'You're twenty-three years old,' an agent said. 'You should be in cracking shape – the best shape of your life.' I could feel one creepy man's eyes on the back of my head and my cheeks flushed bright pink. My hands began to feel sweaty. Was this it? Was my modelling career over before it had really begun?

'You need to get to your goal weight in the next month or so,' they said. 'You have to take this seriously. As you're not working much in London, let's see if other countries suit you better. And in the meantime perhaps you should get a part-time job.'

As a model, your agency will 'place' you with different agencies abroad so that you can work in foreign markets. Each fashion market has its own beauty ideals, which means girls may work more in one city than another based on their body type or appearance. For example, New York and Paris are considered high fashion – skinny, tall runway girls. London has all the cool and edgy girls (and sadly I don't think I was interesting enough to make an impression, even with my wonky teeth).

In fact, because of how much of a misfit I was, no one seemed to know where to place me, even abroad.

One Monday afternoon, I had a meeting with an agent from Miami, where the beauty standard is busty, toned beach babes. I was a pale, flat-chested, skinny white girl.

That Friday, the same week, I met a Japanese modelling agent. The looks they wanted couldn't have been more different. I had pale skin and big eyes, which they seemed to like, but the moment he put the measuring tape around my hips I realized how much of a waste of time this was. He smiled at me patronizingly, swiftly moving on to the next girl.

*

It's hard trying to hide the fact you're making yourself sick from someone you live with, especially someone who likes things neat and tidy. I'd rush through food as though I'd never have another meal again, eating and eating and eating until I felt physically sick. Then I'd go upstairs to the bathroom, turn the shower on and position it in the bath so that the noise of the water drowned out the sound, then would stick two fingers down my throat until every last bit of food had gone. Every time I threw up I'd inspect the toilet bowl rigorously, making sure the remnants of the last meal I'd eaten weren't splattered about the place. Then I'd wipe away my tears and check my eyes didn't look red, brush my teeth and head downstairs again, pretending everything was all right.

I couldn't stop. Throwing up as a means of de-stressing was part of my routine now. A bitchy comment from my agency, a bad casting, arguments with Scott, wishing my parents were nearby, worrying about a potential job or lack of money . . . it would all disappear in a blink of an eye (well, blink of a *BLEURGH!*). I was losing grip of my life more and more.

Want to know how much control I had over my career? A friend of mine messaged me on Facebook, congratulating me on my new signing to a Parisian modelling agency. Huh?

'I think you've got the wrong person!' I wrote back. But then he sent me a link straight from the French agency's Facebook page: a giant photo of my face, with the words,

'BLAH BLAH BLAH CHARLI HOWARD BLAH BLAH' written underneath it (I don't speak a word of French). What the hell was going on?!

I confronted my London agency about it the next day.

'Oh yeah, you'll be going over there soon,' a booker said, totally unbothered. 'They're one of the biggest agencies out there. It's a great thing. They really like you.'

'But . . . but . . . shouldn't we have discussed this first?' I asked. My anxiety began to calculate the worst possible scenarios that could happen.

'I thought you'd be happy,' she scoffed in an attempt to make it look like I was being ungrateful.

Then another booker piped up. 'You're also signed to an agency in Denmark and in Stockholm.'

If this doesn't prove how much of a commodity I was, I don't know what does. I was a human being who just wanted to be on top of what was happening in her life, and I was being treated like an object.

Paris was, without a shadow of a doubt, the worst place I have ever, ever, *ever* modelled in. Yes, it's a nice city, full of culture and fit men, and, yes, these days I am partial to a good old croissant or macaron from time to time, but the body image standards over there are nigh on impossible to meet. Some model friends told me that when it came to weight, you could never be thin enough for these agencies. This, I'd later discover, was true.

I was given a week's notice about my trip to Paris and, while we're not exactly talking Australia here, it was my first solo trip away from home – or, more specifically, Scott. How was I going to cope without him for three whole weeks?!

I had no clue where I'd be staying or what I'd be doing while I was there. None of this was explained to me. A good agent will tell you what your schedule is like and what is expected on your trip away. But not mine. Every time I dared question where I was staying, I was made to feel that I was p*ssing them off or being a nuisance. Want to know how this helped my anxiety? Oh yeah – it didn't.

'What do I wear in Paris?' I remember asking beforehand.

One of the bookers sighed. 'Black,' she replied, not looking up from her computer. 'Just lots of black.'

So, with this knowledge, I went to H&M and bought a few black things with what I could afford – bearing in mind I had practically no money in my bank account to live on for three weeks; at most, I had £150. I didn't know if the clothes I'd picked were any good or not, but they were black, so they must've been OK. Right?

Because my anxiety was through the roof, and because I was beyond stressed, my skin broke out. So then I ended up stressing myself out more, worrying what the French agency would say about me when I arrived.

Well, this time, it turned out that I was right to be worried.

I got into Paris at around 10 a.m., having been up since 5 a.m. to get the Eurostar from King's Cross. It was a boiling-hot day in June and the start of Men's Fashion

Week, so I had coincidentally been sitting next to a male model on my way there, who was trying to give me the lowdown on what to expect. Safe to say, he wasn't really selling it. Once I arrived at the station, I got a text from one of the French bookers, saying he'd meet me at the end of the platform.

'Ah, *bonjour*!' I heard a voice say. It was my French booker – and he was lovely. He made a couple of phone calls in French, which I assume were to say I'd actually arrived and hadn't legged it, and we set off on the Metro to the French agency, making small talk.

As we walked through the door, the most horrifically anorexic woman walked past me, floating by like some sort of Dementor from Harry Potter. Her legs were as wide as my arms, her cheekbones like razor blades. I was *awestruck*.

'That's one of ze bookers,' my new friend whispered, and he guided me through into the main office while I tried to pull my jaw off the floor. Despite the fact I *knew* she was terribly ill and needed to be sectioned – her arms looked like they could snap off at any second, and any hint of muscle or fat had dissolved completely – I couldn't help but envy her. How on earth did she maintain the willpower to stay that thin? How many calories must she eat a day? I know that sounds sick, but, hey, I was sick myself.

'*Bonjour!*' another man said, double-kissing me on the cheeks, and then he eyed me up and down, his eyes narrowed in curiosity. His name was Victor, and I later discovered that he was the head of the women's board. A bossy older lady came out and did the same thing, then they started muttering away in French. I was rather glad I didn't understand what they were saying, as judging by their facial expressions I'm sure it wasn't pleasant. I didn't need to be a mind reader to see they weren't pleased with the thing that stood in front of them.

Still, despite the fact my heart wanted TO RIP OUT OF MY CHEST, I kept smiling. I didn't want them to latch on to how insecure and nervous I was, despite the fact I could now feel beads of sweat around my hairline.

Victor got out a measuring tape in the middle of a busy office and measured my waist and hips.

'Sirty-six,' he said, tutting, and suddenly I felt like I was in trouble. Thirty-six? I could've sworn my hips measured thirty-five inches. That's what my latest modelling card in London said I was anyway.

'Zis is not good,' he said. 'You need to be sirty-four. In France we like . . . we like . . . *thin.*'

'Oh, right,' I replied, pretending this was the first time I'd heard such a thing.

Victor sighed loudly. 'You need to lose two inches in a week,' he said, without batting an eyelid. I was waiting for the punchline to drop, but nope – he was deadly serious. I'd massively wasted his time. But come on! Two inches? Was he mad? Did he know I'd been struggling to lose that for a *year*?!

'I don't think that's possible,' I replied honestly.

'It is possible,' he said. 'I know girls who do zis.'

'O . . . kay . . .' I replied slowly, debating whether or not I was the delusional one. Then he started to get mad, his voice getting louder.

'I am angry at your London agency!' he said in this big office full of people. 'You are too big for Paris. Why 'av they sent you 'ere, when your 'ips are a sirty-six?! You cannot work!'

I felt like such a huge disappointment. In all honesty I didn't know why my London agency had sent me here, either, and truly wished they hadn't. I already hated it, and I'd barely been in the country an hour.

Victor emailed my agency in front of me, typing furiously. Soon my phone rang.

'Why are your hips thirty-six inches?!' the London booker asked furiously.

'I . . . I don't know,' I replied.

'For God's sake,' she said. 'How have your hips gone *up* in size? He's saying there's no point in you being there.' There was a pause. 'I must admit, you didn't *look* like you were a thirty-six when I saw you the other day . . . but then again I probably should've measured you.' I couldn't help but think if my hips didn't look thirty-six inches, why was it a problem? Another pause. 'Victor's saying you should probably leave Paris at the end of this week, but he's not sure. He's going to feel it out. Oh well. You might as well give it your best shot.'

In that moment I hoped I gained a ton of weight so I'd never have to deal with these French arseholes again. It was my first spark of defiance. People with anxiety need certainty, and while modelling probably wasn't the best career for someone craving consistency I felt I at least deserved to know when I could or couldn't go home.

Without a clue about how to use the Metro and with barely any money, I made my way to the model apartment, which was up a very steep hill in a posh part of Paris, using a printed-out map. Had I known my account was due to be charged eighty-five euros a night for staying there, I would've just got a hotel. But I didn't know this, because NONE OF THIS WAS EXPLAINED TO ME.

Thankfully, I had a room to myself, but there was an extra bed in there should another girl come and stay. I desperately hoped I wouldn't have to share my room with a stranger. Two of the other rooms in the apartment were occupied by other girls, but I had yet to meet them.

I was unpacking my things when I heard the front door open. *Clip, clop, clip, clop.* The bedroom door next to me slammed shut, and I suddenly heard a loud sobbing. I could make out a Spanish voice, which soon turned into epic wails and yelling. I couldn't help but burst out crying, too. I wanted to go home.

Still, there was no time to feel sorry for myself. I had a casting across the other side of town to get to: French *Elle*, which I was pretty sure I wouldn't get based on the comments I'd received earlier.

I managed to get to the casting in the nick of time. I sat on the floor in a corridor clutching my new portfolio, next to beautiful girls who were ten times prettier, taller and thinner than I'd ever be. When I flicked through the photos,

I noticed they'd picked the pictures where my bones were most visible, or where I looked thinnest. I scowled at my model cards, which lied and said my hips were thirty-four inches (wishful thinking, eh?), and hoped this was all just a very bad, very depressing dream.

It wasn't a dream. It was a bloody nightmare. As the days rolled on, and I did a couple of shoots and incessant running to and from castings, no one could tell me whether I was coming or going. Victor kept telling me how many castings he'd had to cancel because of my 'weight problem' (his words, not mine), yet he couldn't tell me if I should go back to London early or not. I think he genuinely believed I could lose those two inches in a week and didn't want to book my return trip home in the hope the miraculous would happen – that I would be perfect.

He said that he'd told some big French brands that I'd come down with the flu, but that I would see them when I was 'feeling better'. Looking fat, apparently, was worse than being ill. I'd call my London agency about coming home early and they'd say, 'Talk to Victor about when you should leave,' or not answer my emails at all. I was in total limbo.

The day of my so-called departure came, and it became quite apparent that I wasn't leaving. I was in such a bad mood. I just wanted to go home. In fact, I told Victor there was no point in me being there, and he got defensive, asking why I wasn't taking my stay in Paris seriously enough. I couldn't win!

He may have cancelled some castings because of how 'fat' I was, but over the period of the next two weeks I kept going to huge castings for the biggest French magazines and brands. It should've been a dream come true, yet this wasn't how I'd envisioned my dreams unfolding. Victor couldn't hide his surprise when a few of the clients actually optioned me for things (which is when a client keeps you on hold for that job as a potential model). This pleased me secretly. It meant people thought I had something. It meant I couldn't have been the troll he was making me out to be.

In a twist of fate Victor and I gradually seemed to like each other. Not in a romantic kind of way, but as . . . well . . . friends, almost. He would tell me my hips were big each and every time I saw him, but aside from that he wasn't *too* bad. Despite the cultural barrier, he thought I was funny, telling me how much he liked me and how he just *knew* I was going to land huge campaigns one day. I began to feel like I could be cheeky around him, despite the fact I was shy and introverted with my agency in London. Perhaps this was down to the fact I'd stopped caring or taking the job too seriously, just like when I used to play up in school.

Funny things happen when you stop caring too much what other people think.

On my *actual* last day – which, by the way, may have been the happiest day of my life – he gave me a big hug and told me he'd see me soon. *Yeah, right*, I thought to myself. *I'm never coming back here again.*

'I don't want to go to Paris again,' I announced to my London agency the minute I got back. They agreed. They bitched about Victor and the agency for a bit, saying how weird he was and how ridiculous the French modelling standards were (which is funny, because theirs were just as bad), then told me I didn't have to go again.

Three weeks later, they told me I'd been booked for a big hair campaign in France, and that I needed to stay in Paris for another two to three weeks; they couldn't be certain for how long. So much for never having to go back, eh?

'How long do I need to stay for? Is it two weeks, or three?' I said nervously, frustrated that yet again no one could give me a straight answer.

'I don't know. You'll find out once you get there.' That was all the information I was given, and my stomach churned, worrying about whether I would, once again, look too fat.

This job was worth 3,000 euros. Want to know how much I got from it? Nothing. Nope, not a cent. By the time you added up the costs from my stay at the model apartment, my new portfolio and cards, and the massive cut the agencies took from my earnings, I was actually *indebted* to them instead. What a great start!

This was just one of a few French jobs I didn't see a single penny from, not to mention I would be treated quite terribly during them. I was made to feel like a prude for not wanting to go topless. People ignored me, speaking French around me.

Once, on a scorching hot Parisian day, I almost fainted on a shoot. I hadn't eaten properly since lunchtime the day before, unless you count two squares of dark chocolate 'dinner'. The photographer ran over to me and held me up by the arms while the make-up artist fetched me water.

'Are you OK?' he asked, fanning me with his hands. I smiled meekly, sipping water.

'You look great, though,' he said, showing me the screen of the camera. I suppose he was right. For the first time ever, my chest and collar bones were prominent. Even the Brain Deviant was impressed.

My latest model apartment wasn't as nice as the last one. For starters, I was sharing a room with a bulimic fifteen-year-old model from Norway. The most unsettling thing for me was the fact this girl was out partying with nightclub promoters and men in their thirties every night. The only real communication I'd have with her was when she'd come in every night at 1 a.m. after clubbing, and we'd whisper 'hi' to one another.

Each day was the same. She'd wake up, get dressed, starve herself throughout the day and then go partying in the evening. They'd wine and dine her before plying her with more alcohol and taking her to creepy clubs. The room smelled like sick because she'd throw up the meals afterwards, either in the bin or the bathroom next door.

I felt sorry for her and the fact she was bulimic. I took Victor aside, telling him about this girl and how wrong it was that gross old men were taking her out every night, but it wasn't like he cared. He didn't care when I told him she was making herself sick, either. The weirdest thing about me confiding in him was that even though I knew I was making myself throw up as a means of stress-relief and weight loss, I still couldn't see I had a problem, too.

Maybe it was down to stress or the constant running to and from castings, but as the months continued back in London, I had begun to lose a bit more weight. I was sent to Paris frequently, continuing to rack up more and more debt and not booking any jobs. Now when I sat down, there was a large gap between my thighs. I'd ogle at this thigh gap, mesmerized, standing up and sitting back down again to see if it really existed, yet still managed to convince myself I was obese.

Victor noticed it, too. It's a weird feeling, being congratulated on losing weight you don't actually need to lose, with the level of excitement appropriate for if you'd just cured AIDS.

I was strolling through Paris one afternoon when Victor called me up. He was so excited that I didn't understand a word he was saying. I asked him to speak slowly.

'You need to come to ze agency!' he said. 'Ze biggest casting director has asked to see your pictures!'

'Can't we do it another time?' I asked. I never felt good enough for Polaroids. As well as taking photographs, for which I'd have to deliberately position my body in a way to appear thinner, these sessions were also an excuse to measure me again to check I hadn't gained weight. I was being measured once a week by this point and the experience never left me feeling warm and fuzzy.

'No!' he snapped. 'Come in now!' And, just like that, he hung up the phone.

Reluctantly, I made my way to the agency. It was another hot Parisian day, muggy and sticky, and I had to sanitize my hands a good couple of times before arriving at the building. I could practically feel the germs crawling over me, though in hindsight it was probably just insecurities swarming my body instead.

He took the photos enthusiastically this time, going on and on and *on* about how amazing this supposed casting director was. I really didn't care any more. I was too hungry to think straight. Then, as I'd predicted, he took out my arch nemesis, Mr Measuring Tape, and measured my hips.

'Ah, *bon*! Just one more inch, and you will be *parfait*!' he said happily.

I left the agency in two minds. One half of me wanted to keep dieting so that I'd become *'parfait'* like Victor wanted. The other half wanted to curl up in a ball and hide away.

For the first time since developing an eating disorder I finally felt thin. I was now seven and a half stone, dangerously underweight – just what I'd always wanted. I caught sight of my reflection in a shop window, and couldn't believe how small my thighs looked. It didn't even look like me. My thighs no longer touched as I walked, just like I'd dreamt of. People looked at me on the Eurostar back to London with a mixture of shock and sympathy. And even though I'd finally achieved my goal weight – something I'd worked towards for almost ten years – I still wasn't happy. I suppose that now I'd achieved my dream: I was finally learning that happiness was not found on the scales.

*

It wasn't just my agency that had weird obsessions with weight and body image. When I say it was an industry problem, that's what it was.

I finally booked a hair campaign, which are great jobs to land as they pay a lot of money. Although it was a relatively hot day, I was still wearing layers of clothes to keep warm. My hands and feet were like ice blocks, a sign of malnutrition. I'd made myself sick the night before in order to look svelte for the photos, and had already drunk copious amounts of tea to rid any water weight and to give me an extra boost of energy.

The make-up artist that day wasn't very personable or friendly, unless you happened to be one of the married men on set. Clearly not one for girl power, she pretty much disregarded all of the other women on the team, including the director of this international hair chain. She was very successful and had worked with many of the world's biggest celebrities. Apparently, that meant she could treat people however she wanted. She'd click her fingers at an assistant, asking them to get her a coffee, then began screaming at them when they didn't put the right amount of milk in it.

I was having my photos taken when she came over to me on set and patted her stomach in front of everyone. 'Make sure you suck this in,' she said, then waltzed off.

'I beg your pardon?' the female director said, and the room fell silent.

'I'm telling her she needs to get rid of her tum–'

'I heard exactly what you said. She hasn't got a tummy to suck in,' the director spat.

You could have cut the atmosphere with a knife. Who knew my tummy could cause such an uproar? The make-up artist looked at me as though it was all my fault, then stormed off.

'You're perfect, and don't let anyone tell you otherwise,' the director said, and we got back to shooting. It was amazing to have another woman stick up for me like that, and I've never forgotten it.

Another time, I was booked to shoot a lookbook for an up-and-coming designer. There were barely any snacks or any food on set all day. Lunchtime came, and one of the assistants rushed off to get cheap sandwiches from a local supermarket, dumping them on a spare table.

I was *hangry* by this point. My legs were shaking, my stomach rumbling. I knew I couldn't eat the sandwich, because not only would I get severe stomach pains from the gluten, but I'd also bloat out significantly and ruin the photos. The designer had conveniently whisked herself and her team to a nearby posh restaurant, leaving me and the make-up artist alone with packets of junk.

But what else could I eat? There was nothing else available. I opened a couple of sandwich packets and scraped the fillings into my hand. Buttery slices of ham and scrapings of tuna don't make a great meal, in case you were wondering. I began doing the arithmetic in my head, working out if I'd gone over my calorie allowance for the day.

Lunchtime ended, and it was back to business. I was seething by this point. All of a sudden, a very frail girl arrived.

'Who's this?' the make-up artist asked the designer curiously. 'I didn't know we'd be using another model today.'

The designer turned her back to me, as though by doing that, I'd somehow lose my hearing. 'She'll be modelling the swimwear,' she replied, unbothered. 'Charli's too curvy for that.'

I was just a UK size six. But the other model was easily a size zero – smaller and more perfect than I'd ever be.

An email appeared in my inbox out of the blue announcing one of the agents had left the agency. My heart dropped. While I wasn't working all the time like some girls were (the lucky gits), the one woman who booked all the jobs I did get had just upped and left with no explanation whatsoever.

Don't get me wrong, someone from the agency had to go; the atmosphere had been horrendous for a while. You didn't have to be a genius to see the agency was divided down the middle, both figuratively speaking and literally. Three people sat on one side of the large office desk, gossiping and bitching, while the head of the agency and another booker sat on the other.

The agency went through interns and assistants like nothing else, who, by the way, were treated appallingly. According to one model, even the head of the agency ran out of the office crying once.

Still, I wasn't expecting this particular agent to leave. Whether I trusted her fully or not, she was booking girls jobs worth hundreds of thousands of pounds, huge fashion campaigns and the best magazines. She'd always told me I'd get there one day, but now she'd left I wasn't sure I ever would.

That evening, I spoke to her on the phone. I'd texted her to ask where she'd gone, but, like she usually did, she got me to call her so nothing was written down. It turns out she had left to go to a different, already established agency. She'd grown tired of feeling like she was doing all the work, and, according to her, the agency hadn't been growing in the way she wanted it to.

She was subtly hinting that the agency would fail without her there. And I believed her

'You can come with me if you want,' she said towards the end of the conversation.

How could I possibly say no?

Unfortunately, I couldn't just up and leave the agency like I wanted. Because I'd been so blinded by the prospect of fame and fortune, I'd hastily skimmed the contract I'd signed when I first joined the agency without studying it properly. (I don't need to tell you what a stupid mistake that was to make.) As part of my contract, I had a three-month notice period, which meant I couldn't sign with any other agency until that time was up. Not surprisingly, the head wouldn't let me leave early, and I had to wait those three months out.

I did absolutely bugger all for those three months while I waited to be freed from my contract. Hours turned into days, where the smallest of tasks, like food shopping or going for a run, became incredibly difficult. It would take me an hour to get ready to leave the house, my mind a jumbled, foggy mess. I'd trail through the new agency's website on my laptop, watching all the girls I knew move over to join her.

In order to pass the time, I decided to organize a couple of shoots myself. I'd always admired the beauty of the old fifties film stars, their perfectly curled hair and voluptuous bodies, and wanted to do a shoot where I looked the same (well, wishful thinking). Even though their bodies were in complete contrast to mine, and despite the fact that the Brain Deviant told me thin was the only way to look beautiful, I would've died to have had an ounce of their beauty.

The shoot was so much fun. The hair, the make-up, the clothes: I looked womanly and I *loved* it. I learnt to pose my body in a 'curvier' way, emphasizing my shape. When I got the photos back and posted them to Instagram, they got more likes and comments than any shoot I'd ever done. My skinnier photos never had the same response.

But looking curvy wasn't acceptable for models. And so, as always, I went back to starving myself in preparation for the new agency. But as the waiting around became more and more unbearable, for the first time ever I started to think about quitting altogether. So why didn't I? There was absolutely nothing binding me to modelling. It wasn't like I was a slave, was it? I'd chosen to go down this route – no one had coerced me into following it through this far. But here's the problem I now faced. After modelling for over two and a half years, there was a huge gap on my CV. No one wanted to hire me.

Modelling was all I had.

12

GETTING A BACKBONE

It was a freezing-cold day in December when I finally made my way to the new agency. My hands were blue and purple, my nose was running, and the concealer on my face was either cracking or coming off. This was the first time I'd be seeing my agent in three months, and to say I was worried about it was an understatement. God, I hoped I hadn't put on weight.

I tried topping up my make-up, sitting on a wall outside the agency, hoping they couldn't see me out of the window. Any attempt to hide blemishes or purple skin wasn't working. *Sigh*. Too late now. This was it. I made my way into the new office, and put on a smile.

'Hello, darling!' They greeted me excitedly, giving me hugs. I could feel their eyes inspecting me.

'Right, let's update your measurements,' said an intern I hadn't met before. She didn't say a word as she measured the tape round my boobs and all the way down to my hips.

The mood suddenly became irritable, and continued to get worse by the time the camera appeared for Polaroids. Sensing the change, I was trying to be upbeat and chatty, but it was quite apparent this wasn't going well.

'Sort your hair out,' someone said. 'Rough it up a bit.' I did as I was told. I was trying to relax, but that's easier said than done with people glaring at you snidely from across the room.

'I don't get what's happened,' a booker said, scrolling through my images on the camera afterwards. 'You look so bloated. You can do so much better than this.'

'I'm a size six, though,' I replied. I'd never really spoken back before. Where did that come from?

'It's not about size. It's about *this*,' she said, and patted her tummy. God – I bloody KNEW I shouldn't have had that sandwich two days ago! Bloody GLUTEN! BLOODY SCOTT ENCOURAGING ME TO EAT IT WHEN I SAID I DIDN'T WANT IT! Where was my willpower? Why wasn't I capable of doing the simplest of tasks?!

'I'm disappointed,' she said, which was handy, because that's precisely how I felt, too.

This was all my fault. Nobody had forced me to eat. I had nobody to blame for this bloating other than myself. Losing weight should've been easy . . . so why wasn't it? Why was losing weight so damn hard, despite the fact I was only eating 1,000 calories a day?

I left without signing a contract. I was told that I should spend the Christmas holidays getting back into shape, and that someone would call me the day the office reopened. Well, what a ho-ho-horrific time that Christmas would be. I guess I'd have to cut down on the pigs in blankets – and then some.

Christmas came and went; joyful and merry it was not. Scott and I spent the majority of it arguing. We were engaged by this point, though the idea of actually having to marry this guy was stressing me out even more. I'd hide my engagement ring in the bathroom cupboard, hoping it would make the prospect disappear – running away from my problems like I always did.

And then January the first came. The next week came. So did the week after that. By the end of the month there was still no news from the agency. Although I was waiting around for their phone call like some kind of needy puppy, there was a huge part of me that didn't want to hear from them.

The month was almost over, and so, without having had a single call or email, I assumed I wouldn't be hearing from them again. Some of my friends had moved over with my agent too and I'd heard rumours that they felt they'd made a huge mistake.

And then, just as the month came to a close, a message appeared in my inbox. It was from my old agency. They'd been bought out by a huge American agency, and gained a whole new staff.

You should come in and see us, it read.

What did I have to lose?

*

It was the same location, same office, but it felt fresher, somehow: a new beginning, with new staff and new ideas. Only two of the old staff remained – the head and another booker, both of whom welcomed me into the office with a smile and open arms. All the other staff were new, and they seemed friendly enough. A new intern rushed to get me a cup of tea.

I realized I'd have to sit there and eat humble pie after walking out just a couple of months earlier. I felt like a right prat. They seemed OK about it all, though.

'Honestly, they were *awful*,' the head said, sitting in the exact same spot she had the first time I'd signed with her. 'They were so horrible about girls behind their backs, throwing things at them as they walked out of the door.'

She accidentally confirmed that one of the creepy bookers had been absolutely vile about me behind my back, and while one half of me was happy my anxiety hadn't made this up, it also made me feel uncomfortable, knowing he'd bitched about me. 'I never understood why he was so vindictive towards you, or said all those horrible things. He was *awful*.' Why hadn't she stood up for me then?

But any doubts I felt were shoved aside by the excitement I felt at working with the name of the massive American company the agency was now part of. I'd always had dreams of going to America to model, but I'd always been told the likelihood of that happening was . . . well . . . zero. I was too short, too big, too imperfect. Now that they were part of this huge American brand, working over there seemed within reach. Despite my anxiety, I had what it took – I just *knew* it. The head told me all the plans for the agency and the plans for taking it forward. It sounded so exciting.

'I have one request though,' I said.

'Go on.'

'In my photos on Instagram, I'm finding people are responding well to my curvier pictures,' I said. 'Whenever I post those pictures, I get way more likes. So I think we should make my book go down that direction.'

'Love it!' she said. 'Yep, let's go down that direction.'

Was I hearing this right?! Someone wanted to represent me *for me*?! I put off signing a contract (I didn't want to risk a three-month probation if I were to leave again) but within a couple of hours I was back up on their website. It was time to move on to bigger things.

I was practically skipping home that evening back to Scott, when, as though some sort of joke, I got a text from the other agency. My heart sank.

When are you coming in to see us? Xxx, it read.

I'm not, I replied.

My phone rang.

'What the hell do you mean, you're not coming back? Where have you gone?!'

I said the name of the agency, which didn't go down very well.

But I was done being a pushover.

'I waited for a month for you to call,' I said. 'I'm sorry, but no. I'm done.'

*

The first couple of months at the new-but-old agency were great. It was February, i.e. fashion month, and although I never usually worked during this time as I wasn't a catwalk model, I was being booked for brands I would have never expected. OK, they weren't Burberry, exactly, but I was earning money here and there, working with bigger and better photographers. I'd made the right choice, I was sure of it!

I was given a chance to work with a new photographer to get new photos for my portfolio. It was meant to be a sexy shoot, in order to promote the new shape that the agency had allegedly been keen to promote, and I spent the day feeling incredibly anxious.

I knew I looked fat. I could see it in the mirror. I'd been up since 7 a.m. downing litres of water in the hope of flushing out any 'fat' and extra water weight I may have had. My tummy growled from having eaten nothing since lunchtime the day before. I wanted to look sexy and womanly, and yet at the same time I didn't. I could be curvy, but not too curvy. I couldn't let go of the obsessive thoughts about thinness.

'Please can you Photoshop me thinner?' I begged the photographer afterwards. I'll never forget the look on his face as he realized I wasn't joking.

'What? There's nothing of you . . .' he said.

'My cheekbones aren't defined,' I replied. 'Please. I can't let my agency think I've put on weight.'

'I'm not Photoshopping you,' he said. 'I might get rid of a spot or two but I'm not slimming your body.'

*

Sure enough, two days later, I got a call from the agency. It was one of the bookers, and she wasn't in a good mood.

'We need you to come in and measure you to see that you're not as big as the photos suggest.'

I made my way into central London, trembling. They were going to drop me, I just knew it. Why couldn't I be thin?! No matter how much I fought my body, nothing was changing.

She measured my hips and my waist.

'Hmm,' she said. 'That's weird. You're smaller. Must've been a bad angle. Keep toning up, yeah?'

I found the photos recently. The last time I saw them was with my anorexic mindset, where I was viewing someone ten times bigger. Looking at them now, I realize I wasn't 'big' at all. My arms look like they could snap off, my legs are wasting away. I appreciate that my self-image was insane. But I was being encouraged in that behaviour.

The work . . . well . . . stopped. I worked once, maybe two months after that for a famous jewellery brand, but that was it.

I wasn't scared of not working. I was scared of what would happen to my mind when I didn't. When I was sitting at home doing nothing, my thoughts began to consume me. Anxious, I rang up one of my new bookers to ask what was happening.

'Should I be worried?' I asked, which was funny, because I already was. 'I haven't worked in weeks now.'

'I'm trying to be honest,' she said, which is a polite way of excusing yourself for being rude, 'but you've got to tone up more.' Tone up, as I'm sure you've gathered by now, means to 'lose weight'. 'You'll get so much more work that way.'

'How much do I need to lose?'

'Ideally, you'd have a thirty-four hip,' she said. 'But it's mainly just looking as tight as possible. The tighter you are, the smaller you'll fit into the clothes.'

'OK,' I replied. 'It's just that when I came in January, you guys said we would push me down the curvier route. I'm never going to have a thirty-four-inch hip.'

'It's just the industry, babe,' she said. 'You know what it's like. I'm not saying starve yourself, but you need to be small. That's the way it is.'

She sent me an email an hour after the phone call, along the lines of: *Hope I didn't upset you earlier! We just want you to do the best you can xxx*

Yeah, yeah, blah, blah, blah. I'd heard that line many times before. This wasn't beneficial to me in the slightest. Me not lining my stomach lined their pockets.

Not at all! :) xxx, I replied. It didn't matter anyway. My anxiety was back.

'I can definitely see a difference,' the booker said as she took photos in my lingerie a few weeks later. 'I can definitely see more definition.'

My heart leapt. I'd been exercising two hours a day in the gym, running until I could no longer walk properly. I was barely eating anything, and if I'd ever had a problem with salt or gluten before, this was like nothing else. If vegetables had salt on them, I would freak out. I'd have a smoothie in the morning and for dinner, then some poached eggs for lunch. My diet was so strict, so *precise*, and it was driving Scott mad.

'Keep going, and you'll be great!' the booker said.

My heart sank. For crying out loud – how good was good enough? I was so tired of never being perfect.

When I got my photos back, however, I was quite impressed by how toned I looked. Although it didn't translate in the mirror in my head, I had abs. I looked better than I ever had. But I wasn't thin. Worst of all, I'd clearly been Photoshopped to look thinner for clients – the picture frames behind me were wonky from where they'd edited it badly.

I posted them on Instagram, but an hour or so later I had convinced myself I was fat and deleted them. Other models would probably laugh at how obese I looked. No wonder I didn't get any jobs.

I kept dieting – or, more precisely, starving myself – and the workload didn't miraculously improve like I believed it would. Yet again, I was thin, but still didn't believe I was thin enough by fashion standards. At twenty-four I was a woman. My hips weren't designed to be super thin, and never had been. And yet I kept believing that by dieting I would eventually get to that size. Why – oh *why* – couldn't I be thin?

I was also broke. I mean, I'd been poor since leaving school, but I was truly skint at this point. I couldn't complain – this was a life I'd chosen for myself, and if the money wasn't there, that was no one's fault bar my own. I was holding out for my fairy-tale ending, the one big job that would turn my life around. In the meantime I got a job working on a brownie stall. Yes, that's right – I got a job selling chocolate brownies to punters across the south of London. For an anorexic, this wasn't exactly easy work. Imagine a drug addict serving people heroin every day. It would be torture. But I was making seven pounds an hour, which was all right when all you're doing is serving tea and brownies. Told you modelling was glamorous.

But this experience was great for me. Because I was having to deal with people hands on, I was starting to build up confidence. I began looking people in the eye. But you know what was weird? As I developed confidence, this made Scott feel uneasy. It was as though he liked me when I was insecure, but when I was having a fun time he didn't like it. For example, I remember booking a job with a world-famous photographer and rather than getting excited he told me 'not to get too big-headed' about it.

I didn't fancy Scott any more. He was my friend who knew every secret (well, bar the bulimia, of course), but I no longer respected him.

Every night, I would continually be nagged at: the dishes weren't clean enough, the shoes weren't by the front door, there was an unopened letter on the side. I didn't really care any more, though. I knew that whatever I did wouldn't be good enough.

I'd always been interested in working in the media, and now that I was regaining confidence at the brownie stall, I wanted to push myself more.

All the way over in west London, a charity was holding courses for people under twenty-five looking to break into the media. It was run by an amazing woman who'd been a famous TV presenter in the 90s, and who had a lot of well-known friends in the industry. We were going to be taken to Google, to the BBC, to the Discovery Channel and shown how to get into presenting. Aside from modelling, nothing had seemed so appealing to me before.

I had barely been at the agency for five months, but that didn't mean I didn't refresh my inbox religiously in the hope the email of my dreams would randomly land in my inbox. By this stage, it was though I didn't exist. My portfolio was never updated. I never went on any castings. One of the bookers came to my brownie stall and that was slightly awkward, trying to look model-worthy with chocolate crumbs smeared down my shirt.

Part of the deal with the media course was that you committed to all the days. But my anxiety still played up. What if I applied and then a modelling job came up? What would I do then?! But the rational side of me also said to give this course a go. I could no longer sit at home all day doing nothing. I had to do something with my life.

The course was wonderful. It was one of the best things I've ever done. I made friends from different backgrounds, all of whom wanted more for their lives. We met famous news reporters and celebrities. And you know what? People liked me for *me*. They didn't care about Modelling Charli. They liked me for who I was.

Although it's safe to say I was far from an ideal student, I'd always been told I was a good writer in school, and the media course made me wonder if I'd like to pursue it as a career. I had no idea how to get into writing. But then, by chance, there was a competition the first week of the course to see a new up-and-coming rapper called Stormzy, and so I wrote my best piece of work and won. I got to take a new course-mate with me to watch him in Camden in the press area. It was like attending school, except I was good at it and never got into trouble. I did have a brain, after all.

With my modelling 'career' now lurking in the background, I started to ease off the worries about my weight. But then I got an email four weeks into my course telling me I'd been booked on an e-comm job in Scandinavia for £1,800. Wow! That was more money than I'd made in a while. My period was due, and I had a couple of spots on my chin. But, hey, everything is Photoshopped, and I assumed it would be fine. I flew out there, slept overnight, and the following morning got to work.

Well, let me tell you, e-comm work is boring AF. I shot over eighty different outfits that day, and while that isn't exactly working down the mines, it was still tiresome. But then I was handed a pair of leather trousers to put on. I tried squeezing into them, but the button wouldn't do up. Have you ever tried putting on leather trousers? There's no stretch to them whatsoever!

Not to worry, I thought. *They're the one item that hasn't fit me today.*

The woman on the shoot was p*ssed off by this stage. 'Why don't they fit?!' she said irritably. Don't get me wrong, it was an awfully long day. We were all exhausted. But because the leather trousers didn't fit, a particular shot she wanted was ruined.

But that was it, so I thought. The pictures were great, so the photographer herself told me, and I flew back to London feeling pleased with myself.

But then a couple of days later I received an email from the agency. They wanted me to come in and see them. This time I knew my paranoia wasn't playing tricks on me. My gut instinct told me this was it: that my modelling career was over, and I was going to be dropped.

Well, let's look at the facts. This recent job was the only one I'd had in months. Every time I'd been in to see them I'd been told I wasn't small enough. The last time I'd visited them, which was about eight weeks before, I'd had to go in for Polaroids while on my period.

'Can I please do them another day?' I'd asked nervously. 'I don't feel my best and I'm a bit bloated.' That's normal, right? I mean, who the hell wants to be photographed in their bra and knickers when they're bleeding out of their vajayjay?!

'No, we need these ASAP,' they said.

And so I went in for the photos. This was so pointless, as any definition I had from the gym was now covered by squishy water weight. But they took the photos as per usual, and then at the end proceeded to tell me how 'bloated' I looked.

'I did tell you that,' I said. 'I was on my period.'

I'd never seen them so p*ssed off with me before. They told me what I was doing wasn't good enough. 'You have to lose the inches,' one booker said. 'This is ridiculous. It's like you don't care.'

I did care – more than anyone realized. I wanted to do so well at modelling, but no one could see the lengths I was going to in order to achieve it.

And so, since Period Gate, the work had completely stopped. I was being made to feel bad, and all because my body didn't look in top shape due to a bodily function. I was being made to feel bad for *being a woman*.

Then I got a call to see my agent. I definitely wasn't going to go into an agency to be dropped in a room full of people. That would be mortifying. Instead, I rang her up from the toilets instead during lunch.

'You wanted to chat,' I said.

'Oh . . . yeah, right,' she said. 'Oh. Well, this is going to be a bit awkward!'

What – like dropping me from the agency in person wouldn't be worse?!

'Look . . . we've all had a chat, and we don't feel this is working,' she said. 'We got told by the Scandinavian client that you were too big to fit into the clothes. We really appreciate how much work you're putting in to getting in shape, but you're just never going to be small enough.'

I didn't know what to say. I was a size six. I'd never been thinner. To a doctor, I would be underweight. To say I could *never* get into shape was the biggest insult I'd had to date.

'Maybe you should go down a different route? Modelling isn't for everyone. It works for some people; for others it doesn't. Some people's bodies are designed to look like models, and others aren't. I know you said you were doing a media course at the moment – perhaps you could look into that more ...? It's really nothing personal, but sometimes these things happen. Anyway, I hope we can still be friends!'

I came out of the toilets dumbstruck. A couple of girls approached me, asking what was wrong.

'I've been dropped by my agency. For being "too big".'

The looks on their faces were priceless.

I tried not to cry as they wrapped me up into a group hug. I just wanted to go home.

This was my biggest fear, and it had come true. I'd been told I was too curvy to ever be perfect.

But instead of being devastated I was ... angry?

It had taken till this moment for me to realize something. I'd spent my life catering my body to fashion's standards ... but wasn't fashion supposed to cater to *me*?! Aside from being a consumer, I was also a *human being*. When did it become acceptable for women to starve themselves to fit a dress size, just because one random guy decided that was the way women should look? When was beauty defined by a number?

Along with the entire fashion industry, I was to blame for encouraging these unrealistic expectations for women. Rather than put my foot down, I allowed these standards to dictate to me what was beautiful. I dieted, excessively. I bought clothes because they made me look thinner, rather than better. And in the process of wanting to become someone I wasn't – someone I'd never be – I'd lost touch with who I was.

Once upon a time, I was happy. I was a girl with big dreams and a big mouth. And that old me seemed like a different person altogether. Modelling didn't cause me to develop eating disorders – those were already there, lingering in the back of my mind – but it certainly fuelled them. Fashion gave me reasoning behind my madness, leading me to believe that by being thinner I'd be accepted by the elite.

I was tired of being tired, tired of having no money, no social life, no certainty and never feeling good enough. I also knew I was never going to recover from my eating disorders if I kept allowing myself to follow the beauty advice of people whose ideals were so far-fetched you might as well be reading a fairy tale.

I sat on this news for a day or so. Don't get me wrong – my anxiety was awful, but only because I was thinking about what I'd do now that my dreams were over. My media course finished in a couple of days, and I was well and truly back to the beginning.

There was one thing I was certain about, though.

There suddenly seemed to be a lot more to life than being thin.

I'd written the Facebook post on the Tube home, after my sadness had turned to anger. Who the hell did these people think they were?! It was easy for these bookers to sit there and judge me from their office desks, not realizing just how much work I was putting in every day.

This is what it said.

Here's a big F*CK YOU to my (now ex) model agency, for saying that at 5' 8" tall and a UK size 6–8 , I'm "too big" and "out of shape" to work in the fashion industry.

I will no longer allow you to dictate to me what's wrong with my looks and what I need to change in order to be "beautiful" (like losing one f***ing inch off my hips), in the hope it might force you to find me work.

I refuse to feel ashamed and upset on a daily basis for not meeting your ridiculous, unattainable beauty standards, whilst you sit at a desk all day, shovelling cakes and biscuits down your throats and slagging me and my friends off about our appearance. The more you force us to lose weight and be small, the more designers have to make clothes to fit our sizes, and the more young girls are being made ill. It's no longer an image I choose to represent.

In case you hadn't realized, I am a woman. I am human. I cannot miraculously shave my hip bones down, just to fit into a sample size piece of clothing or to meet "agency standards". I have fought nature for a long time, because you've deemed my body shape too "curvaceous", but I have recently began to love my shape. I don't have big boobs, but my bum is ok :) plus, a large majority of my clients are ok with this.

And anyway, let's face the facts: when I was 7 and a half stone,
I still wasn't thin enough for you. When I went to the gym
5 hours a week, you still weren't finding me work. I can't win.

Ironically, I do love modelling – the people I've met, the
places I've visited and I am proud of the jobs I've done. I will
continue to do it, but only on my terms. My mental and
physical health is of more importance than a number on a
scale, however much you wish to emphasize this.

If an agency wishes to represent me for myself, my body &
the WOMAN I've become, give me a call. Until then, I'm off
to Nando's.

It wasn't just aimed at them, either: it was aimed at everyone
who had ever made me feel fat or worthless. I was done. I
never wanted to model again. And then I clicked 'post'.

My phone was blowing up left, right and centre. People
were calling me, either to tell me how funny what I'd
written was, or that I should take it down. But I refused to.
I'd finally had enough.

My post began getting shared. By that evening alone it
had been shared about two hundred times. I hadn't realized
how many women, models or not, had felt the pressures of
trying to become thin. This was a problem that had affected
women the world over. Although my eating disorders had
frequently made me feel alone, I saw how so many of us
had struggled.

Suddenly, now I *didn't* have an agency, I was everywhere:
daytime telly, *The Times*, the *Daily Mail*. It must've been a

slow news day. My Facebook post had gone viral. People saw me across the world, from Italy to Pakistan.

I thought I could handle this attention, but I was finding it hard to. It was like I was having an out-of-body experience. I was contacted by hundreds of journalists to give a statement. I went from having 6,000 followers on Instagram to 20,000 in a week.

I was too scared to go on TV, but the woman who ran my course said I should do it to help other people. And so I did. More and more messages flooded in from girls who'd all been through the same thing: girls who were literally on their death beds from anorexia being told to diet; girls who, like me, bought fashion magazines and who became ill trying to emulate the models. I wasn't alone. People were on my side.

This attention lasted for about a week. On day two, I was contacted by an agency in New York, Muse, asking if I could call them. *No way*, I thought. *I'm not going down that route again.*

But out of interest I decided to google this agency and was surprised by what I saw. They were huge, yes, representing some of the world's biggest fashion models, but they also had a curve division – beautiful girls who were landing huge jobs, but who had tits and an arse. I'd always been a bit snooty towards curve models – I never considered them 'real models' – but the jobs these girls were getting in New York proved me wrong.

Within a few days, I signed a contract and they flew me out there. My new life had begun.

13

MY FAIRY-TALE ENDING
(FOR REAL, THIS TIME)

I had been in New York for a week and a half and I was anxious as hell, swamped by such a huge city. Although this was a massive deal for me, Scott and his parents were putting pressure on me to fly back to London earlier than I wanted for a family birthday party, so I didn't feel I could relax. This was my fresh start, and yet it felt Scott didn't want it for me. (Turns out I was right – he didn't.)

I was totally overcome that an agency as wonderful as Muse wanted to represent me. I expected them to drop me at any moment, coming to their senses. They had girls shooting campaigns for the likes of Chloe, Gucci, Louis Vuitton, Marc Jacobs, and shooting spreads for *Vogue*, *Elle* and all the other major magazines. It all seemed too good to be true. Too good for me, anyhow.

I was completely overwhelmed with how my life had taken such a sudden turn. I'd gone from being dropped by an agency in London to being flown out to New York – the one place they told me I'd never make it – within two weeks. What the hell was happening?!

The day I stepped into my New York agency for the first time, I came across a small section of model cards hanging on the wall in the curve division. I'd met a couple of curve models back in England, but – and I'm ashamed to say it – I never took them seriously. Well, why would I? No one took *me* seriously if I gained so much as an inch. And so, rather ignorantly, I'd always assumed any models who had a bit of extra flesh weren't model material, either.

Except these girls *were* modelling. The jobs they were booking spoke for themselves: they'd modelled for the world's biggest brands and magazines, and their photos were high-end and high fashion. It seemed ludicrous to me that some of these girls were considered plus-size when they were smaller than most girls you saw in the street. Although they were bigger than me, I didn't think they were any less attractive than I was. They were a million times more beautiful – their bodies were so sexy and womanly. And despite what I'd been led to believe my entire modelling career, their curves weren't a deterrent, but a selling point.

What also stood out to me was the fact these girls were smiling on their comp cards – not in a cheesy kind of way, but in a natural way because they weren't starving themselves, which I suppose makes everyone cheery. Everyone is happier when they're allowed a pizza or two, aren't they? And here these girls were, getting to model, while actually ENJOYING it. What a *dream*! I couldn't help but feel envious.

But I wasn't here in New York as a curve model – I was here to, once again, work as a 'straight-sized' model. And this time, the competition would be harder than ever before: I would truly be up against the elite. New York is the biggest and most competitive market for models, and if you can make it there, you can make it anywhere.

The thought of having to maintain a small body size again stressed me out. My mind began racing, repeatedly telling me I'd be dropped if I gained the teeniest bit of weight. And I was so desperate not to let anyone down that I felt the stress more than ever.

Remember how I said I didn't remember the first time I'd made myself sick? Well, I certainly remember the last. The Brain Deviant had been bombarding me with stressful thoughts, from navigating a new city to being pressured to fly back early by Scott, worrying I was morbidly obese, and having no money. The second week into my stay, I'd been invited out for dinner by an old school friend from Hamburg, who'd offered to show me around New York. That's one good thing about moving a lot, I suppose – you have friends across the world to call on.

He took me to a lovely restaurant in an expensive neighbourhood, and on the way there I walked past a pet shop with puppies in the window. Oh God, how cruel! Were they all right in there?! It broke my heart seeing them pawing at the glass. One more worry to add to my list.

With the thought of these puppies fresh on my mind, I sat down and ordered a burger and chips, which I thought would be culturally appropriate in the land of fried food. I wanted this old friend to see I could enjoy food like a normal human being, except of course my mind was calculating all the calories in the dishes. No alcohol; I stuck to water. (I couldn't risk any more calories being digested, could I?)

When the burger came I took a huge bite into it. OH MY GOD. It was *delicious*. I'd go so far to say it was the best burger I'd ever had in my life, but this was coming from someone who hadn't eaten a burger or bread in over two years, so perhaps I wasn't the best person to judge.

But then, right on cue, the Brain Deviant kicked in.

'*CONGRATULATIONS, YOU FAT F*CK!!!*' it yelled. '*YOU WILL HAVE GAINED A STONE FROM THAT BURGER!!! WHERE'S YOUR WILLPOWER?! WHY WOULD YOU HAVE A BURGER, WHEN YOU'VE BEEN OFFERED THE BIGGEST OPPORTUNITY OF YOUR LIFE TO MODEL IN NEW YORK?!!*'

'Are you OK?' my friend asked. 'You seem a bit quiet.'

'Yeah, fine!' I lied.

In actual fact I'd begun to internally panic, my hands dripping with sweat. The Brain Deviant was right. I'd been given this amazing opportunity, and when I next went in to Muse they were bound to drop me for the overnight weight gain. All because I couldn't control my cravings.

I finished the burger in record time, racing it down until I could barely breathe, then excused myself to go to the loo. God, even the toilets looked like something out of The Ritz – perfect navy blue octagonal tiles everywhere and gold finishings. Not that it mattered: it would be splattered with my sick within minutes.

My throat hurt as I kept ramming two fingers down my throat. My nails were sharp. Images of the puppies in the window kept flashing up, then images of me looking fat, fat, fat from that stupid-but-oh-so-delicious burger. I imagined how great I'd feel once the sick had left my system; how clean and pure I'd feel . . .

Mascara ran down my face as though I'd dunked my head underwater. My eyes were red and bloodshot. I grabbed toilet paper and scrubbed the surfaces ferociously, feeling bad for spoiling such a beautiful interior. God, what must people think?

As I walked back to the table I hoped the dim light in the restaurant would somehow hide the abysmal physical state I was now in. We got the bill, my eyes not reaching my friend's in the hope he wouldn't notice anything different. Experience taught me the bloodshot eyes would fade in a few minutes anyway.

As we said our goodbyes and I headed home the usual relaxed feeling I'd get after being sick hadn't arrived. I held my head in my hands on the subway. This wasn't normal. Throwing up a lovely (and expensive) meal wasn't normal. This way of dealing with stress WAS NOT NORMAL.

I knew I needed help. I didn't want to be this way any more. But you can't just shake off eating disorders or low self-esteem.

They don't just disappear. My fairy-tale ending had come . . . and yet it didn't feel like it. Why didn't I feel calm? Why didn't I feel content with the opportunity I'd been given?

When I got home, I started crying. I cried that night and I cried in the morning. Once I'd calmed down and stopped being so irrational, I decided to do what I should have done a long time ago – call my parents and tell them I had a problem.

There were two reasons why I'd never sought help for my bulimia before. First, I thought people would think I was attention-seeking, especially my parents, and being referred to as bulimic would've been mortifying to me. Secondly, I'd always maintained what I was doing was OK, because it was my secret.

The sentence 'I've been making myself sick since I was fourteen' blurted out of my mouth like . . . well . . . word vomit. This sense of relief was like nothing I'd ever experienced before. And you know what? Rather than yell at me or call me attention-seeking, which is what the Brain Deviant made me believe would happen, my parents were AMAZING. I explained how I'd been doing this in secret for ten years now, and how I did it as a means of stress relief because of my nerves. I'd been so good at hiding it that they never knew I'd been struggling.

The following March, I moved to New York for good. What was supposed to be a three-month stay ended up being permanent, as Scott and I broke up. That was a fun time! I'd only been in New York a few weeks when he told me he'd met someone else. Don't worry, though – once I stopped crying I realized what a blessing in disguise that was. He was holding me back from achieving my dreams, happy to live an average life, and now I was ready to put myself, my health and my career first.

Having said that, it wasn't easy pretending I didn't have an eating disorder. I still very much did. People kept calling me 'brave' for talking about my treatment by my ex-agency, asking me if I'd ever had an eating disorder, and suddenly I felt on the spot and ashamed. I wasn't ready to talk about it yet. I hoped that if I didn't speak about it, people might stop asking.

As much as I wanted to model I desperately wanted to be free from my demons, too. After years of battling food I was finally ready to get better. That's the thing with eating disorders – you need to want to get better yourself. No one can make that decision for you. Besides, I was happy in New York. I didn't want a repeat of Paris, where I ate nothing for days. I wanted to enjoy myself. I was jealous of other people having social lives and going out with friends, eating and drinking like *normal* people did. Why couldn't I be the same?

I'd gradually come to the realization that I wasn't as fat as I thought. Or that I was, but deep down I actually knew that I wasn't. Does that make sense? No, of course it doesn't, but that's anorexia for you. You're completely delusional. One minute your body looks thin, the next it's morbidly obese. I would close my eyes and mutter, '*I am not fat, I am not fat*,' as though that would somehow change the distorted view I saw in the mirror . . . and yet it didn't. But something told me that if I kept telling myself I wasn't fat, eventually I'd believe it.

Becoming a curvy model did not happen overnight. Nor did getting better. But I knew I couldn't throw up any more. Instead, if I got the overwhelming urge to 'clean myself' (as I liked to call it), I would do something else to distract from those thoughts. A ten-minute shower was all I needed for the thoughts to drift away. I was stronger than this illness. I just knew it.

Meanwhile, the curve board at Muse was doing better and better. I watched intently as the fashion industry began taking notice of curvier girls. They were landing bigger campaigns and magazine editorials, and gradually the board was getting bigger. Becca, the head of the curve division, genuinely believes in fashion being more diverse, and listening to her talk about the change needed was truly refreshing to hear.

Between moving to America and trying to battle my demons, without realizing, I'd slowly begun putting on weight. This now left me in a tricky spot. My body didn't seem to fit in either of the markets. As I put on weight, I now faced the problem of being too big to work as a straight-sized model, and too small to fit the curve. I would turn up to castings and people would question why the hell I was there, or not even see me at all.

I didn't fit in anywhere. I'd be on hold for jobs that would fall through last minute – so near, yet so far. That first year, I only worked a couple of times, and yet despite my concerns Muse said they weren't going to drop me. They believed in me when I didn't believe in myself, refusing to let go.

Despite the lack of work, day by day, my happiness was growing. This might sound a bit dramatic, but the last time I'd ever felt this content was as an eight-year-old at my dodgy primary. So much of this new-found happiness came from food and the fact I was upping my calorie intake. Nothing bad happened if I ate a few potatoes at dinner or cereal in the morning. Nothing bad happened if I didn't exercise that day, or if I had an afternoon snack. I was starting to see food as a friend, as nourishing, and not my worst enemy.

Towards the end of that first year in New York, I landed a make-up campaign with one of the world's biggest brands. It was a dream come true to see my face splashed across the New York subways and the internet. By this stage, I was a UK size ten and, after having thrown away my measuring tapes, weird calorie-counting notebooks and scales, I hadn't been taking note of my weight.

It was lovely seeing how supportive Muse were. And then I noticed Becca, who wasn't my direct agent at the time, had shared my new campaign online.

Her caption read something along the lines of how great it was that curve girls can also land make-up campaigns. My heart stopped. Me? *Curvy?!* All the negative connotations I had with that word suddenly came to the forefront of my mind. Damn, I must've gained weight – noticeably.

But when I studied the video properly, I *was* curvy. She was right. I had a tummy. My thighs were bigger. And so what? What was so bad about that? It didn't make me any more or less attractive. The make-up brand clearly didn't think I resembled Shrek, hence why they'd booked me for the campaign. Besides, I'd spent the last year envying the careers and lives of the models on the curve board, so why was I worried?! It was a compliment, if anything. I'd kill to look like some of the models on there.

Like the time I first nit-picked my flaws and everything that was 'wrong' with my body as a teenager, I locked the bathroom door that night, stood in front of the mirror and dropped my clothes to my feet. Yes, I *had* gained weight. My thighs weren't completely smooth, and I had some cellulite on the backs of them. My upper arms jiggled a bit. My cheekbones weren't as defined. And . . . so what? Did it make me a worse person? Did it make me less pretty? Did it make people like me any less?!

NO!

Of course it didn't. I was still the same person. I'd put on weight and the world hadn't come crashing down. I'd faced my worst fear and beaten it. I may have gained weight, but I'd also gained other things: happiness, regular periods, clear skin, shiny hair, a social life.

I finally understood that being thin wasn't worth it.

At a size ten, I was well and truly an 'in-between'-sized model, not fitting either modelling category. In fact, I was not only the sole girl at Muse my size, but also among most modelling agencies. Unlike most curve girls, my face was quite angular, while my body was womanly and squishy. I noticed that a lot of curve brands were optioning me for things, but I never got the job because I was too small for them. Overall, I was getting optioned for more curve brands than I was 'straight-sized' ones. And so I knew I could either own this 'unique' trait of mine, celebrating what made me unique, or give up modelling altogether.

One afternoon, I went to meet Becca in Starbucks and asked if I could join the curve board. I was finally ready to embrace my true shape.

'Welcome to the fun side of modelling,' Becca said as I signed my contract.

It was around the same time as this that I met another curve model in a cafe in Brooklyn. Becca had suggested we meet up as we were both starting to embrace the body-positive movement.

I'd had an idea for a while of shooting a high-end editorial using a variety of body shapes, but didn't know where to begin. I knew that seeing images like that when I was a teenager dreaming of modelling could have changed my relationship with my shape. So considering my body type didn't seem to fit in anywhere, what would be better than creating fashion images where it *would*? As the saying goes: if the door won't open, create a new one. Or something.

Anyway, I knew I shouldn't have to eat a ton of food or excessively diet just to be taken seriously as a model. Not only that, but why was there such a divide between straight-sized models and curve models? They were never photographed together, as though it was shameful for one to be seen with the other. You were either thin or fat and nothing in between.

There had been some body-positive campaigns before, but they were – in the politest term – *bloody tacky*. Curve models were always shot as jolly and sexy, never high-end or tomboy. On the other hand, skinny models were never photographed as womanly or curvaceous – it was as though photographers deliberately tried to shoot them as thin as possible. These images certainly didn't represent a lot of women, especially not those *buying* the fashion, and turned women's bodies into caricatures. Everyone has a different idea of what makes a model; a size shouldn't determine that.

Since joining the curve board, I had learnt that ALL bodies are beautiful in their own way. God, what a cliché, but it's true. There is beauty in every body, from a lithe body with protruding bones, to a woman with curves and rolls. The media loves to divide women as it is – the last thing we need is to body-shame each other. So why not shoot images in which female bodies were celebrated and brought together? Doesn't everyone deserve to be represented?

Funnily enough, the model I met for coffee also wanted to create a fashion editorial with the same kind of vibe. We spoke about our ideas and the All Woman Project was born.

We'd scout models who had something else going on in their lives, from music to art to motherhood, proving they were more than just pretty faces. Our other idea was to make the shoot completely female-led, from the photographer to the stylist to the designers to the videographer. No one knows how to shoot or dress women better than women, right? So that's what we did. It was A LOT of work, and not everyone was behind the idea at first, but the team we gathered made it all so worthwhile.

One of the looks we were shooting was all the models together in colourful swimsuits. I was terrified of being shot in a bikini, still trying to embrace my body and new-found curves. But as I stood there on set with girls of all different shapes, sizes and colours, I didn't feel like a freak. I saw girls thinner than me with stretch marks and confident larger girls who owned their bodies. What was there to be ashamed about?!

The final photos were beautiful. I cried when I first saw them. They were precisely the pictures I wish I'd seen growing up. No one looked cheap or tacky; the models looked like goddesses. The images were exactly what fashion should be: inclusive and diverse, without losing its 'fantasy' appeal. Oh, and they were completely genuine – we didn't edit out a single thing. Not many fashion images can say that, let me tell you!

Not surprisingly, the photos went viral very quickly, being picked up by news publications worldwide. Women from around the world messaged us, telling us how confident we'd made them feel. Who'd have thought some diverse photos could've had that effect? Well, fashion holds more influence on women's body image and self-worth than I think it likes to take responsibility for.

I truly believe that women will always be fascinated by other women, and that a model wearing a size bigger won't make them want to buy a product any less. It's all about the photography, make-up and styling, and allowing the consumer to escape into a dream world. That's what fashion is about after all, right? Allowing people to dream, like so many of us do. A dress size should not prevent girls from dreaming.

Not long after our campaign, body-positive fashion campaigns began springing up out of nowhere. Within a year, we saw fewer white, tall, skinny models in images, and instead there was a more diverse cast.

There's still a long way to go, but something wonderful happened. It became cool to be different.

THE END

And so this is where my story ends.

In case you're wondering, I'm still a bit mental. I'm still a bit of a misfit. But that's OK. Being mad has allowed me to share my story, and doing that helped me to recover from my eating disorders. I've learnt that talking openly about my problems doesn't make me a weak person, nor does it anyone else.

Yep – it's only taken me twenty-odd years, but I am pleased to tell you that I have embraced my curves, well and truly. I actually *like* my squish; I like the things that make me womanly. If you'd told me, aged fourteen, that I could be a model as *well* as curvaceous I would've spat my tea out. In fact, screw that – if you'd told me I'd be curvy AT ALL, I probably would've had a heart attack. Weight gain was the thing I feared most. And yet I embraced my fear, and realized that becoming bigger wasn't bad at all.

I sometimes receive comments from people online calling me 'fat', 'ugly' or 'out of shape'. That would have bothered me, too. But I know I'm not, and that their words are just a reflection of their insecurities. Seriously – is that the best they've got? Is being 'fat' truly the worst thing in the world?! Answer: nope, it isn't. I'd much rather be fat than a bully. And that's what those trolls are.

Muse have never told me to lose weight, and instead encourage me to be the best version of myself. They've done the unimaginable and encouraged me at the size I'm at, which I know I am very lucky to have had. They've booked me huge campaigns and jobs, and I've gone from making seven pounds an hour on a brownie stall to making a real living as a model. I'm living my dream while getting to eat a chocolate digestive when I want to. What could be better than that?!

I know I am lucky. There have been some plus-size models who have accused me of taking their jobs, assuming I have it easier because I'm thinner. Maybe there's an element of truth to that – I don't know. I *do* know a lot of models who'd like to be in my position, but whose agents won't push them at their natural size. I'd love for them to feel content in their job, but the fashion industry still has a long way to go until that happens.

I may have gained a few pounds, but I've gained some other things, too. First off, I've gained a massive dose of self-respect. I no longer let people walk over me. As Eleanor Roosevelt once said, 'No one can make you feel inferior without your consent.' Never has a quote resonated with me quite so much.

Secondly, I've gained the understanding that being kind to myself, both physically and mentally, is a necessity, not a selfish act. I look after my mental health, giving myself time to breathe when I need to.

Finally, rather than solving all my problems, I have realized that being thin was the cause of them. Losing weight does not equal happiness. And I'm proud to no longer contribute to an industry that makes girls feel that way. I'm celebrating the fact that we are *all* misfits, and that the things that make us unique are what make us beautiful.

If *I* of all people can have a fairy-tale ending, anyone can.

EPILOGUE

I read recently that apparently everyone on this planet will suffer with a form of mental illness at some point in their lives. This makes total sense. You don't go through life NEVER experiencing a cold, do you? You don't go through life never getting a bruise or a cut, right? You may get bitten by a snake one day, but there'll be things to treat it if you do. So why wouldn't your brain get a bit 'bruised' from time to time? Doesn't that deserve to be looked after, too?

Your brain is so clever – capable of making big decisions, telling right from wrong, knowing what it likes and dislikes and being able to fall in love – that it may need a bit of maintenance from time to time. Because it works so hard it will become overwhelmed by different chemicals and emotions that it will make the rest of your body feel 'odd' or out of place. So, just like we would a broken leg, we need to mend our heads sometimes, as well.

Over time, I've started to realize that the illnesses I've struggled with don't make me weak or an oddity, but that I definitely don't need to let them rule my life, either.

Pushing problems to the back of your mind is the equivalent of having a tumour and ignoring it until it gets too big to handle. Getting help isn't a sign of weakness. It's a sign that you value yourself enough to treat yourself right.

I wasn't even midway through writing this book when, like an unwanted guest, my anxiety returned. It crept up on me ever so slowly, gathering negative memories, comments and thoughts from my memory bank, before letting all of them off in my head like some sort of bomb.

I didn't get it. This didn't make sense. Writing a book was supposed to be so exciting and special, and yet here I was, riddled and dazed with insecurities and self-doubt. Would anyone like my book? Would anyone even read it?! What would my Amazon reviews say?!! *Aaarrrrgggghhhh!!!*

I was living in the future, too concerned about what people would say about my book, rather than actually living in the present and writing it. I was going to bed at 2 a.m. every night, going over and over and over all the things that could go wrong. My tummy was in knots, sick at the thought of what people would think about it. I couldn't look people in the eye; my hands would be quivering when I handed a cashier change, or if I went into my agency. Then, because I couldn't focus on anything bar my nerves, I couldn't eat. I'd live on caffeine in an attempt to stay focused, but this just made everything worse.

The more I thought about it, the worse it got. Maybe I deserved to fail? Maybe this anxiety was karma for something I'd once said or done? It wasn't just the book I worried about; it was everything. I was ringing my mum up to twelve times a day, asking her if everything in my life would be all right. Modelling, relationships, family. Were my parents proud of me? Would I ever work again? What if my agency dropped me? What if I left the house and got hit by a car? WHAT THEN?!

And that's when I realized I was still running away from my problems, thinking I was big and clever enough to deal with them all alone. Suffering with these things didn't have to be my 'normal'. Who would willingly choose to constantly live in fear over something built up in their brain? You'd have to be crazy to want to do that, rather than want to get better. Besides – how could I end a story about mental health when there wasn't even an ending to what I was going through?!

Anxiety, OCD and eating disorders didn't need to be part of my story any more. You can't control the things that happen or have happened to you. But what you *can* control is the way you handle situations. You can let them make you or break you. And you can also choose whether you want to be happy or not.

I wanted a different ending. I wanted to end this chapter of my life with a new beginning.

And so that's what I did.

Although I was in New York during this time, my mum was a tremendous help. I told her I was struggling, and rather than telling me I was being ridiculous like the Brain

Deviant told me she would, she got on a laptop from the other side of the world and helped to google therapists. I decided to bite the bullet and ring a therapist specializing in Cognitive Behavioural Therapy.

CBT is a way of training your brain into thinking differently – to unlearn what you've already learnt, and to see your thoughts as just thoughts. Rather than telling yourself you're a fat failure, for example, you either tell your inner self to shut up, or push the thought from your mind completely. Most of all, you take a step back and think about the reasoning behind that thought. There's a reason behind every action or anxious thought; we just often forget them. What event or comment triggered you to think so negatively about yourself? OK, that wasn't very nice – time to throw that thought in the bin.

Magical things happen when you stop caring so much about what other people think. Who cares if someone doesn't like you? Is their opinion really the end of the world? Not everyone is going to like you, just like you're never going to like everyone, either. As long as you like yourself, who cares?

I can categorically tell you that you won't reach happiness chasing a low weight or dress size. You won't be happy staying in relationships that aren't going anywhere, or waiting around for people to like or accept you. Running away from your problems won't help you, either.

Happiness is living in the here and now. It is being confident. It is accepting what you look like and who you are. It is being self-aware enough to accept you'll be fine if someone doesn't like you. It is surrounding yourself with people who bring out the best in you, and you in them.

And the most important thing I've learnt about happiness?

There is no such thing as 'normal'.

ACKNOWLEDGEMENTS

Wow . . . a real-life acknowledgements section! Who knew I'd be writing one of these someday?!

I must first thank the hard-working team at Penguin Random House UK for not only letting me write this book, but for also being so supportive with it. To Simon, Tania and the rest of the lovely ladies in the PR and marketing teams; to Wendy Shakespeare and the copy-editors for correcting my grammar (and incessant swearing); to Benjamin Hughes and the art team for a beautiful cover; to the very patient lawyers . . . Thank you for making a childhood ambition of mine come true!

But a huge thank-you must go to my wonderful editor, Holly Harris at Penguin Random House Children's, who has made this whole writing process feel as seamless as it could possibly be. I hope I haven't been too much of a diva! Without you, not only would *Misfit* not have a title, but also wouldn't be here. So thank you for allowing me to share my story (and for making me feel not as mental as I usually do!). You're brilliant.

Acknowledgements

To my literary agent, Adam Gauntlett at PFD, who has been on the receiving end of my anxious emails and phone calls for the past year. Your advice, patience and guidance has been invaluable and I'll be forever grateful for what you've done for me. Let's grab a celebratory lunch (not as wanky as the Groucho) sometime soon.

To 'Mark', for reading through the bits you're in and not demanding I remove them. Sorry for slapping you that time at your party. And for calling you a dick. You're pretty chill now. And you have a good sense of humour.

And same goes to Dave the Woman. There was a time the legal team thought we'd have to change your name to Steve the Woman to help protect your identity, but that doesn't have the same ring to it somehow. Thanks for being cool about letting us use it.

To my Muse NYC family – Conor, Becca, Danielle, Veken, Derek, Jess, Chrissie, Dan, Tara and anyone else I may have forgotten – thank you for believing in me when I've often given up on myself. You've made my dreams come true . . . and then some!

To all the people reading this who might be struggling with an eating disorder or mental health issues. Help is within reach. You can be happy. I chat to many girls on Instagram who struggle with their body image, and allowing us to share our experiences has aided in so much of my recovery. So thank you, thank you, thank you.

And finally, to my family – especially to my mum, who has had to listen to me tirelessly ask for reassurance (thanks,

OCD) for the last twenty years. Thanks for not throttling me at times I'm sure you would have very much liked to. I love you all so much.

xxx

HELPLINES

If you, or someone you know, is struggling with mental health issues, then help is available here in the UK.

I've compiled a list of brilliant helplines dealing with everything from suicide and depression to eating disorders and anxiety. All these helplines are confidential and you can remain anonymous if you wish.

Never be afraid to speak to a parent, relative, friend or doctor about how you're feeling. Getting help does take courage (you know what these Brain Deviants are like), but, in my experience, you'll feel such a sense of relief afterwards. Things can't change if you don't speak up. It really is as simple as that.

MIND

Mind help with mental health, not just eating disorders. I have often visited their website when I've felt depressed or needed help.

Phone: 0300 123 3393

Text: 86463

Website: mind.org.uk

ABC (ANOREXIA AND BULIMIA CARE)
Phone: 03000 11 12 13
Website: anorexiabulimiacare.org.uk

ANXIETY UK
A fantastic charity for people who find life and what it throws at you overwhelming. They're open Monday to Friday, 9:30 a.m. to 5:30 p.m.
Text: 07537 416 905
Phone: 08444 775 774
Website: anxietyuk.org.uk

B-EAT
The UK's biggest eating-disorder charity.
Helpline: 0808 801 0677
Youthline: 0808 801 0711
Website: b-eat.co.uk

SAMARITANS
They listened to me when I was at my lowest. They're open 365 days a year, 24 hours a day.
Phone: 116 123
Website: samaritans.org

MGEDT (MEN GET EATING DISORDERS TOO)
Website: mengetedstoo.co.uk

OVEREATERS ANONYMOUS
Phone: 07000 784 985
Website: oagb.org.uk